GRÉGOIRE NAPI
MIX & REMI:

SWISS HISTORY IN A NUTSHELL

Bergli

About the author and artist:
Grégoire Nappey is a graduate of the University of Lausanne where he specialised in contemporary history. He worked for twenty years as a journalist in French-speaking Switzerland, in particular as chief editor of *Le Matin*. Since 2018, he has been pursuing various activities, including writing, training and communication, including a current assignment as head of communication for *Prométerre*, representing the interests of the agricultural sector of the canton of Vaud.

The drawings of Mix & Remix (Philippe Becquelin, 1958–2016) appeared regularly in the Swiss magazine *L'Hebdo* for three decades, from 1987 to 2016. He also contributed to *Sonntagsblick* and to the French-speaking Swiss television channels. Outside Switzerland, his drawings appeared in *Le Courrier International* and in the magazine *Lire*. He illustrated all the publications in the series *Références* published by *Editions Loisirs et Pédagogie*.

About the translator
After an M.A. in literature from Cambridge in 1960, Robert Middleton has had a varied and distinguished career. Before his retirement in 2003, he was co-ordinator of Tajikistan programmes at the Aga Khan Foundation during the Tajik civil war and is the co-author of the first guidebook to Tajikistan. He is currently mayor of his village in Switzerland.

Acknowledgements by the translator
The translator expresses special thanks to Gordon Read for his eagle-eyed editing, and to Heidi, Félicia and Raphaël for their patience in proofreading.

First published in French with the title *Histoire Suisse*
© LEP Editions Loisirs et Pédagogie SA, Le Mont-sur-Lausanne, 2007
www.editionslep.ch

English edition translated from the French by Robert Middleton
© 2010, 2014 and 2021 Bergli Books, an imprint of Helvetiq, Lausanne/Basel, Switzerland
www.bergli.ch

Printed in the Czech Republic

Bergli is being supported by the Swiss Federal Office of Culture with a structural grant for the years 2021–2025.

ISBN 978-3-905252-19-4

Contents

Introduction

What are Switzerland's origins? What motivated a handful of alpine valleys to form one of the oldest democracies in the world? What was in this region of Europe before the birth of the Confederation? How could a nation be born without being hindered by language barriers?

This book aims to tell – in a clear, condensed and accessible form – what took place on the territory of Switzerland from the first findings of human presence here until today.

The approach is chronological and does not claim to be exhaustive; to make things simple, we have had to make difficult choices and have concentrated on the most important events of Swiss history. Accompanied by maps, a timeline and an index, this history "in a nutshell" aims to highlight the main signposts that will help readers find their way through the various historical periods of this country.

The past influences our everyday lives; an understanding of Switzerland's roots helps to understand how we got to where we are today and how best to face the challenges of the future.

Before Switzerland
(pre-historic to 1291)

Cavemen and lake dwellers
Our ancestors the Celts
Helvetia under the Roman Empire
Religions and languages – their origins
From the Franks to the Holy Roman Empire

A CAVEMAN

A LAKE DWELLER

100,000 B.C. to 800 B.C.

Cavemen and lake dwellers

The earth is about 4.6 billion years old, but humans made their appearance "only" 2.5 million years ago.

During the pre-historic period (before the invention of writing) Switzerland experienced several glacial periods. Humans survived and evolved. As the climate became more temperate, people known as "lacustrians" settled on lake shores.

"Antiquity" followed pre-history. Humans mastered the use of several metals.

Humans arrive on the scene

• The oldest trace of human presence on the territory of Switzerland – a carved stone hand axe discovered in Pratteln (BL) in 1974 – dates from at least 100,000 B.C. Some archaeologists date it as far back as 450,000 B.C. (N.B. for canton abbreviations see pp. 90-91.)

• During the most intense **glacial period** (120,000 to 10,000 B.C.), almost all of Switzerland was covered by a deep layer of ice (around Lausanne it was 1,000m thick). We know, however, that humans and animals (in particular mammoths and woolly rhinoceroses – *Coelodonta antiquitatis*) lived here despite the extreme climate.

In 2002, 700 dinosaur footprints, thought to be 150 million years old, were discovered at Porrentruy (JU). At that time the area had a tropical climate; it was covered by a sea with lagoons and islands.

Neanderthal and Cro-Magnon

Two species of "cavemen" lived in Switzerland:
– Neanderthals (extinct around 35,000 B.C.)
– Cro-Magnon man (Homo sapiens) populated all the inhabitable parts of the globe, the ancestor of modern humans.

Cro-Magnon humans lived in huts, in cave entrances or under rock outcrops. They used tools of bone and flint. Their food came mainly from hunting; they had discovered fire and they buried their dead. Their sculpture and painting are the oldest known human art works.

Agriculture

- At the end of the last glacial era (approx. 10,000 B.C.), the climate became more temperate and Switzerland was covered by immense forests.

- Humans learned to plant crops and farming became widespread. Houses were built of wood. Pottery was made.

  The earliest agriculture was developed in the Near East around 7000 B.C. but took two thousand years to reach Europe.

BOW!
WOW!

The lake dwellers

- Around 4300 B.C., humans settled on the shores of certain lakes, including the lake of Neuchâtel. We call them "lacustrians." There were different phases of lake settlement, sometimes several centuries apart. During these intervals, life continued evolving elsewhere.

- The lake dwellers grew cereals, kept animals, hunted, fished and gathered fruits and plants. They lived in small villages made up of closely packed rows of houses. To protect themselves from high water, these houses were sometimes set on a platform on stilts.

- With demographic growth, the villages expanded and were fortified; agriculture became more extensive. During the **Bronze Age**, from 2500 B.C., bronze, tools, weapons and jewellery were manufactured. Skills became diversified and society became more hierarchical. Some inventions, such as the wheel, facilitated trade. The oldest wheels in Europe (2500 B.C.) were discovered in Zurich harbour and on the banks of the lake of Neuchâtel.

  During the last "lacustrian" period, in approx. 1075 B.C., some villages had as many as several hundred inhabitants. The last sites were abandoned around 800 B.C.

In 1854, excavations for a harbour in Meilen, a village on the shore of Lake Zurich, unearthed a number of wooden poles embedded in the mud. After similar discoveries on other Swiss lakes, archaeologists concluded that the early inhabitants (from 4000 B.C. to 500 B.C.) built their houses on stilts in the water, connecting them with gangplanks. Today, it is generally agreed that the settlements were actually built on land, usually in marshy areas.

800 B.C. to 100 B.C.

Our ancestors the Celts

During the last millennium B.C., the Celts occupied parts of Europe, including the Swiss territory of today.

The Celts comprised different but related peoples who had mastered ironwork. One group, the Helvetii, or Helvetians, settled on the Swiss Plateau* around 100 B.C.

The Helvetians were nomads before the Romans forced them to settle.

* The Swiss (or Central) Plateau constitutes one of the three major land areas of Switzerland (the others are the Jura mountains and the Alps). It covers some 30% of Swiss territory.

The Celts loved fine jewels and beautiful objects. A large bowl of pure gold from the Mediterranean was found near Zurich, indicating the widespread trade relations that existed at that time. However, the Celts did not import everything: four necklaces and five bracelets were found at Erstfeld (UR), the work of skilled local goldsmiths.

Specialists in ironwork

- The inhabitants of the territory of Switzerland during the **Iron Age** (last millennium B.C.) belong to Celtic civilisation, comprising various related peoples living in western and central Europe. The Romans called them *Galli* (Gauls), a general term applied later exclusively to the inhabitants of Gaul – among which were the Helvetians, who came to the territory of Switzerland between 200 and 100 B.C.

The names Nyon, Yverdon, Solothurn and Winterthur are of Celtic origin.

- The Celts were among the first peoples of Europe to work with iron. Widely available, this ore is more difficult to process than bronze, but much more resilient. The Celts made swords and spears of iron and were remarkable warriors.

- The Celts also mastered pottery turning, introduced money and made widespread use of horses.

Religion (the priests were known as "druids") and language were similar in the various Celtic tribes. There were, however, considerable differences in customs and laws.

La Tène

- The second part of the iron age (500 to 50 B.C.) is known as the *La Tène* period, from the name of an archaeological site at the northern end of the lake of Neuchâtel. Excavations there revealed three bridges across the Thièle river, which suggest that this was an important crossing point.

- During this period, the Celts settled throughout Europe. They got as far as Rome, where they were defeated by the Romans in 390 B.C.

BAM! BAM! BAM!

I WAS JUST SAYING THAT EVERYONE WILL GET TO HEAR OF THIS INVENTION !!!

The Helvetians in Switzerland

- The Helvetians were a Celtic people who arrived on the Swiss Plateau between 200 and 100 B.C.

  The Greek philosopher Posidonius (135-50 B.C.) was the first to mention the Helvetians. He described them as "rich in gold but peaceful."

- There are two theories about the settlement of the Helvetians on the present territory of Switzerland. According to the first, they originated in the south of Germany and migrated to the Swiss Plateau. According to the second, the Helvetians occupied an area stretching from southern Germany to the Swiss Plateau from the very beginning.

- In his *Gallic Wars*, Julius Caesar (·····⟩ p. 12) mentioned the Helvetians: four tribes (Tigurini, Verbigeni, Tulingi and Latobrigi) and twelve towns, probably natural sites converted to fortified citadels, similar to that built in a bend of the Aar river near the future city of Bern.

- The Helvetians were at first nomadic. Around 110 B.C., two of the four tribes joined an expedition organised by a Germanic people originating in the north (Cimbri) and left for Gaul (present-day France). In 107 B.C., **Divico**, the chief of one of these tribes, crushed the Romans near Agen (in the south-west of France). Despite some successes, fortune changed sides and the Helvetians had to return to the Swiss Plateau to avoid being massacred.

- Formally, all Helvetians had the same social status, but economic activity allowed some to become richer than others and an aristocracy was formed. They used the Greek alphabet.

  Writing was invented in Mesopotamia (present-day Iraq) and Egypt around 3000 B.C. The Phoenicians (a people originating from the eastern Mediterranean) created an alphabet around 1500 B.C. – it was subsequently improved by the Greeks and Romans, becoming the Latin alphabet we know today.

In addition to the Helvetians, other Celtic peoples settled in Switzerland in the first century B.C.: the Rauracii near Basel, the Sequanii in Ajoie (JU), the Allobroges in Geneva, the Nantuates in the Chablais (VD/VS), the Veragrii in the region of Martigny (VS) and the Sedunii around Sion (VS). The Uberii lived in upper Valais; they are believed to be related to the Raetii, who occupied the eastern part of the country (GR) and were not Celts. The Lepontini lived south of the Alps (TI in particular): they were originally Celtic, but lived under the Romans as early as 200 B.C.

100 B.C. – 476 A.D

Helvetia under the Roman Empire

During their migration, the Helvetians were defeated by the Romans, who colonised the territory of present-day Switzerland.

As a frontier zone of the empire, "Helvetia" gained in strategic importance. The Roman occupation brought prosperity.

The Barbarian invasions forced the Romans out. New peoples moved into Helvetia.

The defeat of the Helvetians

- In the 1st century B.C., the Romans already possessed a huge empire. Geneva was in one of their provinces. It was from here that **Julius Caesar** set off on his conquest of Gaul, where the Helvetians were living.

- In 58 B.C., 368,000 Helvetians (including 92,000 warriors) burned their towns and villages before setting off for the west. Not enough room for expansion? Frightened by the Germanic threat from the north? Nomadic tradition? It is not clear what their motivation was, but their migration marked the beginning of the **Gallic Wars**.

- To reach western Gaul from the Swiss Plateau, the Helvetians tried to pass through Geneva, but Julius Caesar barred their route, pursuing and defeating them in a bloody battle at Bibracte in Burgundy (250km from Geneva). The 110,000 survivors were obliged to return to Helvetia.

- After their defeat, and in exchange for their freedom, the Helvetians agreed to a Roman demand that they guard the frontier in the north of their territory against Germanic invasions. However, this agreement was broken in 52 B.C. when 8000 Helvetians left to support Vercingetorix (chieftain of the Gauls) who was leading the Gallic uprising against Rome. Julius Caesar won this contest and the Romans occupied all the conquered territories, including Helvetia.

From 61 B.C., Orgetorix, a Helvetian nobleman, began preparations for the migration of his people to Gaul. He plotted with other Gallic chieftains to take power as king at this time. But the plot was discovered and Orgetorix was put on trial by his compatriots who did not want a king. He was killed shortly afterwards but his plan for migration was put into effect.

The arrival of the Romans

The colonisation of Helvetia was undertaken progressively. Around 44 B.C., the Romans set up military posts at Nyon (VD) and Augst (BL). Roman garrisons were then placed at other strategic sites.

Around 13 B.C., the Romans conquered the present-day territory of Valais and Graubünden.

A strategic region

- North of Helvetia, on the other side of the Rhine (present-day Germany), lived a group of peoples called Germans. For the Romans, they represented a permanent threat of invasion. After the failure of a campaign in "Germania," the Roman army set up a military post in 16 A.D. on the Rhône, which became a strategic frontier.

- The Roman armies created military camps in Helvetia (e.g. in Windisch, AG). Their presence invigorated the local economy. A road network (Roman roads) was developed.

Helvetia lost its strategic role between 101 and 260 A.D., when Germania was under Roman control and the frontier was pushed further north.

Golden Age and decline

- Helvetia, with its main settlement at Avenches (VD), was easily identified by the culture of its inhabitants: they spoke Latin. The **Pax Romana** encouraged prosperity. The period around 150 A.D. was the golden age of the region. Afterwards, decline set in: the economy slowed down and insecurity returned.

In 275 A.D., the Alamanni, a Germanic people, carried out raids on Helvetian territory. They did not yet create settlements (⸺⸽ p. 15) but destroyed Avenches and Augst.

Roman rule in Helvetia marked the beginning of urban centres in Switzerland: Avenches, Nyon, Augst and Martigny. All had baths and amphitheatres. There were hundreds of agricultural properties on the Plateau, many of which led to the establishment of present-day towns and villages. The road network expanded across the Alpine routes, including the Great St. Bernard pass. Celtic culture acquired Roman features in language, religion, art, social hierarchy, customs, economy and technology. The Romans introduced several novelties to Helvetia: tiles, bricks, plumbing, sewers, nails, cranes, flutes, organs, cats, pigeons and garlic.

- The **Barbarian invasions** brought about the fall of the Roman Empire; foreign peoples (Goths, Vandals, Huns, Franks, Alamanni and others) invaded Europe. The Roman armies were forced to abandon Helvetia in 401 A.D. With the fall of Rome in 476, the territory of Switzerland was occupied by Burgundians (in the west) and Ostrogoths (in the east).

313-550

Religions and languages: the origins

With the fall of the Roman Empire the period known as the Middle Ages began.

Christianity spread in Helvetia. The outer limits of the settlement of new peoples – Burgundians and Alamanni – became the frontiers between the French and German languages.

The Franks gradually came to dominate the whole territory of present-day Switzerland.

In 515, the Burgundian king, Sigismond, founded an abbey on the tomb of St. Maurice in Agaune (today Saint-Maurice, VS).

Maurice was the commander of a Roman legion. Around 300, he and his troops, passing through Valais, refused to renounce their religion. On the orders of the Emperor Maximian, the 6500 legionaries were put to the sword. Myth or reality? Did the martyrdom take place elsewhere but was attributed to Valais? This story is at the origin of one of the most important abbeys of Switzerland.

Christianity – a Roman heritage

- The fall of the Roman Empire marked the end of classical antiquity and the beginning of the Middle Ages. However, despite their conquest of Europe, the Barbarians did not totally destroy the Roman order. Sometimes they assimilated the Roman administration, language or economic system. The main link between classical antiquity and the **Middle Ages**, however, was Christianity.

- Authorised in the Roman Empire from 313 onwards, the Christian religion became official in 391 and gradually spread. The first Barbarian kingdoms followed the trend.

To reinforce his power at the head of the Frankish kingdom, Clovis was baptised at the end of the 5th century.

KING OF THE OPPORTUNISTS IS OUR CLOVIS!

First steps in Helvetia

- Converted Roman soldiers brought Christianity to Helvetia. The first traces of Christianity are found on tombs, holy places and religious objects.

Churches (in Geneva and Martigny) and bishoprics (in Basel, Martigny, Geneva and Chur) were established between 350 and 400.

- In the countryside, pagan (non-Christian) cults sometimes survived. Some holy sites shifted from one religion to another. The conquests by the Alamanni led to a weakening of Christianity in some places.

Missionaries from Gaul founded religious communities – in particular in Saint-Ursanne (JU) and Romainmôtier (VD). The Irish monk Gallus settled south of Lake Constance in 612. The Abbey of St. Gallen was built a century later.

New inhabitants

The Burgundians

From 443, the Burgundians, originating in Denmark, occupied the area of the Lac Léman and the Jura arc.* Not very numerous, they integrated with the local population. They founded a kingdom comprising the west of Switzerland, the Saône basin and the Rhône-Alps region. Geneva was one of its main cities. In 534, the Franks, who were occupying Gaul, conquered the Burgundian kingdom.

* The Jura arc refers to the area along the Jura mountains, extending roughly from Geneva to Basel.

The Alamanni

Established to the east of the Rhine (on part of the present territory of Germany), the Alamanni intended to move west. In 496, however, they were defeated by Clovis, king of the Franks, who incorporated them in his kingdom. From the 6th century, the Alamanni, still under the Franks, began to infiltrate into Swiss territory, taking several centuries before becoming dominant.

Their name is the origin of the French adjective "alémanique" in relation to the German-speaking Swiss.

Rome, Roman, Romanesque, Romansch .... The fourth national language of Switzerland, with a rather Latin sound, is still spoken today in a few valleys of Graubünden. But the slow progression of German goes on and today Romansch struggles more than ever to survive. Only some 35,000 people still speak it.

The origin of the "Rösti-barrier"

("Röstigraben" in German)*

- The Burgundians adopted the language of the peoples in the western Swiss territory: a dialect originating from Vulgar Latin, that became – much later – **French**. The Alamanni progressively imposed the use of a Germanic tongue that is at the root of the "Alemannic" dialects (the ancestors of **German**).

- The frontier between French and German was established only slowly. German stopped at the Sarine river, to the west of which variations of Latin had been most strongly established.

To the south of the Alps, Ticino preserved its Lombard dialect derived from Latin: it was to become modern Italian.

* Rösti is a culinary speciality made of fried grated potatoes and is considered – somewhat dismissively – by the French-speaking Swiss as typical of the German-speaking part of the country.

550-1291

From the Franks to the Holy Roman Empire

Ancient Helvetia was under the domination of the Franks, the ancestors of Charlemagne.

The territory was divided several times between different rulers. At the turn of the millennium, anarchy was followed by a return to order. Dynastic families extended their control and founded towns.

Switzerland came under a new entity: the Holy Roman Empire.

In 563, Lac Léman was the scene of a kind of Tsunami. A mountain called Tauredunum (perhaps the Grammont in the Chablais region) collapsed on to a fortified town (perhaps Le Bouveret at the southernmost end of the lake) and into the lake itself. This created a huge wave that caused much damage and cost many lives. Even Geneva was affected: its bridge was destroyed and many people were killed.

The Frankish period

- Around 550, the Franks annexed Rhaetia (Graubünden) and thereby took control of the whole territory of Switzerland (they had conquered the former Burgundian inhabitants a few years earlier). The 7th and 8th centuries were a time of trouble. The Frankish kings fought for each others' crowns.

- Charlemagne, king of the Franks, who was crowned Emperor of the Romans *(Imperator Romanorum)* in 800, succeeded in centralising power. During the preceding and following periods, however, western Europe was split among different entities. Various territories (empires, kingdoms, duchies, etc.) intertwined. The people were the subjects of local aristocrats (noble families, abbots or bishops); their territories grew or shrank according to their conquests, inheritances and marriages. These conditions meant that there was no such thing as Switzerland at this time.

The end of the first millennium

- At the end of the 9th century, the north-east of Switzerland was under the influence of the Duchy of Swabia, which also occupied southern Germany (Zurich was one of its centres). In 888 the absorption of the western parts into the kingdom of Burgundy (in the east of present-day France) was proclaimed at St. Maurice (VS).

I BET YOU'VE JUST LOST ANOTHER PIECE OF LAND!

- The 10th century was marked in the east by Hungarian invasions (St. Gallen was sacked in 926) and in the west by Moslems from North Africa known as Saracens (the Abbey of St. Maurice was pillaged in 940).

In 972, the monk Bernard of Menthon finally expelled the Saracens. He subsequently founded a hospice on the pass that today bears his name: the Great St. Bernard.

The Holy Roman Empire

- After conquering Italy, **Otto the Great**, king of Germany, had himself crowned Emperor in 962. This was the birth of the Holy Roman Empire. In 1032, all of Switzerland belonged to it.

  In the expression "Holy Roman Empire," "Holy" implies its Christian dimension and "Roman" refers to the earlier Empire of the same name and to its prestigious inheritance.

- This period was marked by less anarchic conditions and by economic, demographic and cultural development. Towns were reborn or created, some of which, such as Zurich and Solothurn, took advantage of the weakness of the Emperor (who had difficulty in imposing his authority) and gained much independence.

The dynastic families

- Several families extended their influence and became very powerful at this time:
  - the **Zähringens** founded Fribourg in 1157 and Bern in 1191; the line ended in 1218;
  - the **Habsburgs** (whose name comes from a castle in Aargau) spread throughout the Alps; several members of the family were elected Holy Roman Emperors; the dynasty played an important role in Swiss history up to the 17th century;
  - the **House of Savoy** established itself between Lac Léman and lower Valais from the end of the 11th century; based at the Castle of Chillon, it took control of the territory of the present-day canton of Vaud through purchase and marriage.

  Around 1260, Prince Pierre of Savoy unified Vaud, which until then had been split into petty fiefdoms.

The castle known as "Habsburg" is in the canton of Aargau. It was built by a noble called Radbot, who, according to legend, gave it the name "Habichtsburg" on return from a hunting expedition when he saw a hawk ("Habicht" in German) perching on its walls. It is, however, more likely that the name comes from the Old High German "hab" or "haw" meaning a "ford", in reference to the castle's role in protecting the river crossing at Altenburg, near Brugg. The castle was built in 1020 but quickly lost its importance for the Habsburgs.Count Rudolf von Habsburg, for example, stayed there only once (in 1256). In 1415, the castle was captured by the Confederates and, when the canton of Aargau was created in 1803 (⸺> p. 46), it became cantonal property and was fully restored.

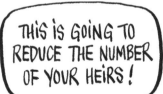

THIS IS GOING TO REDUCE THE NUMBER OF YOUR HEIRS !

cLick!

The foundations
(1291-1516)

The creation of Switzerland
Victories over the Habsburgs
The century of conquests
Marignano: the birth of neutrality

1291

The creation of Switzerland

Three mountain communities joined together to defend their interests and traditions against the Habsburgs.

Although Uri, Schwyz and Unterwalden were allied prior to 1291, the oldest written record of their alliance is dated August of that year. This pact was subsequently recognised as the original founding document of the Swiss Confederation.

The account of three men meeting on the Rütli meadow to swear an oath and the heroic adventures of William Tell are the legends associated with the creation of Switzerland.

The communities of Obwalden and Nidwalden ("above-" and "below-the-forest," respectively) have always been two separate entities and were later to become half-cantons in the Swiss Confederation. In the 13th century, "Unterwald" was used to describe both, but only Nidwalden is mentioned in the Pact of 1291. Later, there was always a common seal for Unterwalden. It appears that only Nidwalden signed the Pact with Uri and Schwyz and that the seal must have been changed subsequently when Obwalden joined the alliance, the date of which is uncertain.

United we stand

- Within the Holy Roman Empire during the 13th century, the Habsburgs controlled Austria and the German-speaking part of present-day Switzerland. Independent communities lived around what is today known as the Lake of Lucerne: their territories were called Uri, Schwyz and Unterwalden (see panel), collectively **Waldstätten** ("forest communities"). In these remote alpine valleys life was hard; good neighbourly relations provided some guarantee of comfort and security. However, their strategic location on important lines of communication awakened the interest of powerful families.

- In order to preserve their prosperity, towns like Bern, Zurich and Lucerne also needed to protect themselves against external threats. For this purpose they sometimes set up confederative associations, of which there were several in Europe from the 13th century onwards.

The Swiss Confederation began among rural communities – towns and town-based political entities only joined later. This was unusual for the period.

The Emperor's favours

- In 1231, Uri opened a transit passage across the Alps via the Gotthard pass, a future strategic axis in the heart of Europe, and obtained so-called "imperial freedom" for the services rendered to the Emperor. This meant that the community was placed directly under the Holy Roman Empire and not under the Habsburgs.

At that time, several towns – but very few rural communities – obtained a special status from the Emperor. Uri was an exception.

- In 1240, Schwyz won its autonomy against the Habsburgs and obtained the protection of the Emperor.

The Pact of 1291 (⋯⟶ Map 1 on p. 38)

- The "forest communities" were already allied prior to 1291. During the 13th century, Uri, Schwyz and Nidwalden concluded a pact of mutual support against external threats.

- In **1291**, Emperor Rudolf I (the first Habsburg to carry the imperial title) attempted to re-establish the Habsburgs' authority over the forest cantons. After his death on 15 July, given the uncertainty over his succession, **Uri, Schwyz** and **Nidwalden** (joined later by **Obwalden**) decided to renew their union and signed a Pact at the beginning of August. This is the oldest known written agreement between the future cantons: it was later to be adopted as the founding instrument of the Swiss Confederation. Today, this document is kept in Schwyz.

UR

SZ

NW

OW

In 1891, on the occasion of the 600th anniversary of the Confederation, 1 August was proclaimed as the Swiss national holiday.

The Pact included the following provisions:
- The forest communities promised "aid, help and assistance," subject to their submission to their "lord" (the emperor).
- Should any conflict arise between the allies, "the wisest citizens of the Confederacy" would mediate.
- Respect for administrative tradition was guaranteed, namely, the refusal to accept the authority of Habsburg officials (known as ministeriales in Latin).
- Judicial cooperation was established: a criminal from Uri was not protected from judgement by fleeing to Schwyz.

The Rütli oath

According to legend, the forest cantons revolted against Habsburg rule. Werner Stauffacher of Schwyz, Walter Fürst of Uri and Arnold von Melchtal of Unterwald, the **"three Swiss,"** accompanied by ten men each, met on a remote meadow – the Rütli – on the shores of what is now called Lake Lucerne. There they vowed to free their lands.

The French- and Italian-speaking Swiss call the meadow "Grütli." It is not known why.

William Tell

There are several different versions of the Tell legend. According to the best known, he refused to pay his respects to the Habsburg coat of arms at Altdorf (UR). Under threat of execution, Gessler, the bailiff (representative) of the Habsburgs, ordered him to shoot with his crossbow at an apple placed on his son's head. Although Tell succeeded in this task, he was arrested. He managed to escape and kill Gessler several days later.

The story of the crossbow and the apple may have come from Scandinavia. It is also possible that real events of the period were transformed into legend.

THE STORY OF WiLLiAM TELL

PEAR VERSiON!

Victories against the Habsburgs

Now united, the forest communities challenged the Habsburgs on the battlefield.

At Morgarten, Sempach and Näfels, simple mountain folk overcame the better-trained soldiers who outnumbered them. Five new members joined the alliance.

Encouraged by their victories, the Confederates strengthened their bonds.

The battle of Morgarten

• After 1291, the conflict continued between the forest communities (defending their autonomy) and the Habsburgs (attempting to control central Switzerland and access to the Gotthard). They clashed in 1315 in Morgarten (south of Zurich).

Some 1500 Confederate troops ambushed and massacred the 3000 to 5000 soldiers of Duke Leopold I of Austria (a Habsburg), who fled in disarray.

• The victory of Morgarten encouraged the forest communities to conclude a new pact in Brunnen (SZ) on 9 December 1315. From now on, they were called the "Eidgenossen" (meaning "those bound by an oath" or "Confederates").

New members (···⟶ Map 2, p. 38)

After the battle of Morgarten, five new cantons joined the Confederation.

In 1339, two crossed white stripes were worn as a distinguishing mark on Bernese soldiers' clothing. The white cross on a red background, a Christian symbol, originated also from the battle flag of the Holy Roman Empire. In 1815, the Federal Pact established the symmetrical white cross on a red background as the official coat of arms. The Swiss flag was defined in its present form in 1889, when the Federal Council decreed that the four branches of the cross were to be one sixth longer than their width.

LU

Lucerne, 1332 – This town, a commercial hub, was in the closest proximity to the Confederates and joined them to preserve its autonomy.

ZH

Zurich, 1351 – Thanks to its silk industry, this town was of major economic importance. To protect its trading access to the Gotthard, it made an alliance with the forest cantons.

GL

Glarus, 1352 – This valley wanted to free itself from the Habsburgs but, not having a mountain pass on its territory, was of no strategic significance. It was accepted into the Confederation, but with a different status from the other members.

ZG

Zug, 1352 – The Confederates took this Habsburg town by siege.

Not long afterwards, the Confederates were obliged to cede Zug and Glarus to the Habsburgs. The forces of Schwyz ousted the Habsburgs from Zug in 1365 and Glarus rejoined the Confederation in 1388 as a result of the battle of Näfels.

BE

Bern, 1353 – As an independent military power, the town had conquered major territories, including the Oberland. It joined the Confederation to guarantee these acquisitions.

Sempach and Näfels

The unifying factor between the Confederates was their common enemy, the Habsburgs, against whom they fought on two further occasions.

The battle of Sempach, 9 July 1386

Lucerne, which had already joined the Confederates, wanted to increase its independence from the Habsburgs. The two camps clashed at Sempach (near Lucerne), where the Habsburgs brought 4000 knights on to the field. But the 1600 Confederates (men from Lucerne and the forest cantons) were victorious, killing 1800 of their enemies, including their leader, Duke Leopold III of Austria.

The battle of Näfels, 9 April 1388

Glarus (which had been a member of the Confederation for a few weeks in 1352) announced its independence. Refusing to accept this, the Habsburgs sent an army of 6500, which clashed at Näfels with the men of Glarus; although reinforced with help from Schwyz, they had only a tenth of the Habsburg numbers. The Swiss won the battle, however, and Glarus became a permanent member of the Confederation.

Arnold Winkelried of Nidwalden is the legendary hero of the battle of Sempach. The Confederates were unable to break through the Austrian lines and Winkelried is reputed to have thrown himself on to the enemy spears with these words: "I am going to open a breach – take care of my wife and children." However, detailed accounts of the battle make no mention of the incident and the first written account only appeared two centuries later. Historians have found proof that Winkelried existed but did not die at Sempach.

New Pacts

• In 1370 (prior to Sempach and Näfels), the cantons controlling the Gotthard (with the exception of Bern and Glarus) concluded a pact known as the "Priests' Charter," which unified their laws and gave equal status to all men before the law.

• In 1393, the "Covenant of Sempach" was signed, the pact between all the cantons confirming the "Priests' Charter." In fact, it was never put into effect but is indicative of the determination of the Swiss to establish common rules, for example to prevent cruelty and lack of discipline in their armed forces.

The remarkable common factor of the battles of Morgarten, Sempach and Näfels is that inferior numbers of mountain people crushed experienced armies without respecting contemporary customs for battlefield behaviour. The Confederates gained the reputation of being valiant warriors, fearless but also capable of brutality.

1393–1477
The century of conquests

The Confederation of eight cantons* acquired more territory.

Swiss warriors were more and more feared in Europe. Allied with France in the Burgundian wars, they played a decisive role in the downfall of Charles the Bold.

But the victors gained little from their successes.

On the battlefield, Schwyz often took the leading role among the Confederates. This is how the local name Schwyz became associated with the whole country. Schwyz became Schweiz in German, Suisse in French, Svizzera in Italian and Svizra in Romansch.

Territorial expansion

Victorious over the Habsburgs, the Confederates confirmed their independence by expanding their territory. They tried to acquire contiguous areas and to control the alpine passes. To this end, they concluded alliances and bought or conquered territory. In just over fifty years, the area of the Confederation increased almost fourfold.

1400   To control the passes to the east of the Gotthard, the Confederates made an alliance with the "Grey Leagues" – three federated entities on the territory of present-day **Graubünden**.

1402   Uri conquered northern **Ticino** (the Levantine valley), the first non-German speaking confederated territory.

1403   Lucerne, Uri, Nidwalden and Obwalden made an alliance with **Valais**, protecting the western flank of the Gotthard.

Valais was then an autonomous bishopric, owing allegiance to the Holy Roman Empire. It slowly became a federal republic (1613) comprising independent districts called "dizains."

1415   The Confederation invaded **Aargau**, which was divided between Bern, Lucerne and Zurich.

1436   After a war against Zurich, Schwyz took control of part of what is today the canton of **St. Gallen** (Toggenburg).

1451   The Confederates concluded an alliance with the town of St. Gallen, and then with **Appenzell** (1452), **Schaffhausen** (1454) and Mulhouse (Alsace, 1466).

1460   The Confederation conquered **Thurgau**.

*Nidwalden and Obwalden are here counted as half-cantons (⤳ p. 90).

HOW TIMES HAVE CHANGED!

BACK THEN, THE SWISS WHERE FARSIGHTED, HAD GRANDIOSE IDEAS AND DIDN'T ALLOW THEMSELVES TO BE PUSHED AROUND!

The Confederates v. the Burgundians

- The Burgundian states, ruled since 1467 by **Charles the Bold**, were situated to the west of the Confederation. They occupied part of present-day France.

- The Confederates were concerned about the growing power of Burgundy, which had invaded Alsace and southern Germany. They made an alliance with Louis XI, king of France, and jointly declared war on Burgundy in 1474.

GOOD THING THESE SWISS ARE GOING TO BE NEUTRAL!

- The Duchy of Savoy, allied to Burgundy, possessed the territory of Vaud, which the Bernese tried to invade in 1475. They were beaten and massacred by the Burgundians at **Grandson** (VD) and forced to retreat.

- A few months later, at Grandson, Bern's Swiss allies came to her rescue and easily put the Burgundians to flight. In 1476, Charles the Bold's troops attempted a new assault but were beaten at **Morat** (FR).

The Burgundian wars were concluded at Nancy, where the French troops, aided by the Confederates, struck a fatal blow to the army of Charles the Bold, who died in this battle (1477).

- At the end of the Burgundian wars, the Swiss acquired new territory:
  - in Vaud, the Bernese occupied the area around Aigle, the first French-speaking territory of the Confederation; contrary to their expectations, they did not get the Franche-Comté, a region now belonging to France;
  - the territory of Valais was extended westwards as far as St. Maurice.

At the end of the 15th century, the Confederation was one of the main military powers in Europe. The Swiss had a reputation for bravery in combat. They were recruited in large numbers as mercenaries in the service of foreign princes. This mercenary service – lasting some 350 years – was an important source of income for rural areas that were often very poor. From time to time, Confederate soldiers confronted one another on the battlefield in foreign wars.

1481-1516

Marignano: emerging neutrality

At the height of their military power, the Swiss had ambitious plans south of the Alps.

Five new members joined the alliance, which now comprised thirteen cantons.* Involved in wars in Italy, the Confederation marched from success to success – but their defeat by France at Marignano marked the end of Swiss conquests.

Switzerland became neutral.

The Diet – the cantons' decision-making body from the 13th century onwards – met in closed session several times a year. Without necessarily gaining in power, its role and composition changed over the centuries. Each state sent one or two senior political leaders to the Diet. Sometimes allied territories such as Valais or Graubünden attended. The requirement for unanimous decision-making (at least for major decisions of principle) frequently complicated the process – already complex because of differences between town and country and between Catholics and Protestants after the Reformation (when separate Diets for each faith were set up).

*Nidwalden and Obwalden are here counted as half-cantons (┄┄┄> p. 90).

Five new members (┄┄> Map 3, p. 39)

FR

SO

Fribourg and Solothurn, 1481 – These two cities had taken part in the Burgundian wars. They requested membership in the Confederation. The rural cantons, however, feared losing their majority. The Diet met at **Stans** (NW). After three years of crisis, Saint Nicholas of Flue, a hermit from Obwalden, negotiated a compromise in 1484 known as "the Covenant of Stans" and Fribourg and Solothurn were admitted.

Federal unity was strengthened. Orbe, Echallens, Morat and Grandson became regions under joint rule (┄┄> p. 34).

Basel and Schaffhausen, 1501 – These two northern towns were already allied with the Confederation and became full members.

Appenzell, 1513 – The valleys of Appenzell, adjoining St. Gallen, were also allies and became the thirteenth canton.

AP*

* At the time, the cantons of Appenzell (┄┄> p. 31) and Basel (┄┄> p. 49) were not divided; the two flags and abbreviations shown here are not official.

Towards independence

In 1499, in the Swabian wars (southern Germany), the Swiss were victorious over the Holy Roman Empire and obtained freedom from their obligations to the emperor – meaning, effectively, independence. However, legal ties with the empire subsisted in Basel, Schaffhausen, St. Gallen and Appenzell until 1648 (┄┄> p. 36).

The wars in Italy

- The control of the alpine passes was an ever-present concern for the Swiss. South of the Gotthard, Uri was already in control of the north of Ticino (the Levantine valley), but wanted to extend its influence as far as Milan. However, it was not alone: several European powers, including France, were staking claims to the Duchy of Milan (Lombardy).

  There were deep differences between the Confederates on the policy to be adopted in Italy. Bern and Zurich – among others – felt that Swiss strategic interests lay not in the south but in the west (the present area of the French-speaking cantons, later known as the Suisse Romande/Welschschweiz).

As night fell on 13 September 1515 at Marignano, Swiss and French forces were forced to suspend hostilities because they could no longer make out which forces were which. They slept alongside one another on the battlefield and continued the next morning by fighting against each other again.

- In 1495, in exchange for the formal support of the Confederates and the supply of mercenaries for an attack on Milan, Louis of Orleans promised Bellinzona, Lugano, Locarno and Arona (today an Italian town) to the Swiss. Five years later, as king of France (Louis XII), he conquered Lombardy, but Uri, Schwyz and Nidwalden only obtained Bellinzona (TI).

- Since the French had not fulfilled their agreement, the Confederates changed sides and, in 1509, allied themselves with France's enemy, Pope Julius II.

- At Novara in 1513, the Swiss crushed the French and obtained the whole of southern Ticino and Domodossola. The Grey Leagues (Graubünden) obtained Valtellina, Bormio and Chiavenna (in the north-eastern part of present-day Italy).

- In 1515, Francois I, the new French king, re-conquered Milan with a powerful army. The Swiss took the field at **Marignano** (south of Milan) on 13-14 September but were defeated by the French.

- In defeat, the Confederation signed in Fribourg in 1516 an "everlasting peace" with France, under which France was given unlimited authorisation to recruit Swiss mercenaries. Territorially, the Swiss retained Ticino (without Domodossola) and Graubünden kept the Valtellina (which is not part of Switzerland today). It was the end of Swiss military supremacy and a first step towards **neutrality**. The Confederation would no longer intervene outside its own frontiers.

An independent country

(1517-1798)

1517-1597

The Reformation

From the beginning, Protestantism spread rapidly in Switzerland.

In several cantons, the Reformation generated opposition to the Catholic Church and became the official religion. The Confederation was torn between the old and the new faith. Civil war broke out.

Despite the Counter-Reformation, four cantons became Protestant, seven remained Catholic and two accepted both faiths.

From the end of the 15th century, Europe enjoyed a cultural and scientific renewal – known as the **Renaissance** – that was to create the conditions for the Reformation. The humanist values of this period were spread thanks to the printing press, invented around 1450 by the German **Johannes Gutenberg**. It marked the end of the Middle Ages.

WE'D BETTER LOOK OUT, OLD CHAP!

THE MIDDLE AGES ARE OVER...

...SINCE YESTERDAY!

The origins

At the start of the 16th century, the Catholic Church was in crisis: there was corruption and enrichment of the senior clergy, priests and sacraments were discredited, the liturgy and religious symbols were obscure and the Bible's message had been forgotten. In Germany in 1517, the monk **Martin Luther** spoke out in favour of a return to the values of the New Testament. His ideas spread rapidly and laid the basis for the Reformation, a religious movement that gave birth to **Protestantism**.

In Switzerland

- Within the Confederation, humanism was very influential and facilitated the spread of Protestantism.

  Humanism is a school of thought centred on man as an agent of free will, and harking back to the ancient origins of civilisation. The Dutch philosopher Erasmus, who taught in Basel, is one of the chief representatives of this school.

- From 1519, **Ulrich Zwingli**, a priest in Zurich, preached in favour of a return to the Word of God (i.e. to the biblical texts). A humanist himself, more radical than Luther, he wanted to make a tabula rasa of Catholicism. After Zwingli won a public debate (*disputatio* in Latin), the Zurich authorities decided to put his ideas into effect.

  In Zurich, between 1521 and 1525, the mass and celibacy for priests were abolished. Zwingli was also opposed to mercenary service, which the Catholics were not.

- The movement spread to Bern, Basel, Schaffhausen and to several of the allies (Bienne, Mulhouse, St. Gallen and part of Graubünden). Glarus and Appenzell accepted both faiths. The towns that had embraced the Reformation concluded a treaty between themselves.

- The old cantons (UR, SZ, NW/OW, LU and ZG), like their ally Valais, remained Catholic and were supported by Austria. Faithful to their traditions, they were hostile to what was happening in the towns. Fribourg and Solothurn also rejected the Reformation and the Confederation was split into different factions; for a while there was no longer a Confederal Diet, but an Assembly of each religious camp.

The two Kappel wars

Despite religious disputes, there was no challenge to the religious sovereignty of the cantons: each chose its camp. However, it was more difficult to agree on the faith to be applied in territories under joint control. The Reformation became a political issue that plunged the Confederation into civil war.

According to legend, during the first Kappel war in 1529, a soldier placed a milk can on the line between the two armies while their leaders were negotiating. Next to it were placed pieces of bread for everyone to help himself. If anyone overstepped the line to take a piece of bread, the other side shouted, "Go and graze on your side!" This story of the "milk soup of Kappel" later served as an illustration, in spite of their divisions, of the strong bonds of brotherhood among the Swiss.

* 1529 – Catholics and Protestants confronted one another at Kappel (frontier between Zurich and Zug). This was the "first Kappel war." Fortunately a compromise was found, preventing battle.

* 1531 – Two years later there was a real battle at the same place. Zwingli wanted to reform the whole Confederation; Zurich, however, militarily isolated, could only apply economic measures by closing its markets to Catholic cantons. The latter reacted by crushing the Zurich troops at Kappel, where Zwingli was killed in battle.

Consequences

* From now on the Diet comprised seven Catholic, four Protestant and two mixed cantons.

* Although fewer in number, the reformed cantons had more inhabitants and their economic importance was greater. This imbalance was the source of disputes between the Confederates.

The Counter-Reformation

* The Catholic Church attempted to block the spread of Protestantism. The Jesuits (the Society of Jesus, a brotherhood devoted essentially to the teaching of the faith) contributed by increasing their influence in education.

In Milan in 1579, Cardinal Charles Borromée founded the Collegium Helveticum, for the purpose of training the Swiss clergy. Declared a saint in 1610, Borromée is revered as the patron of Catholic Switzerland.

* With the Counter-Reformation*, some parts of the country became Catholic again. In Appenzell in 1597, this led to a division of the canton (the Protestant Ausserrhoden and the Catholic Innerrhoden).

AI   AR

* The Counter-Reformation was a period of Catholic revival beginning with the Council of Trent (1545–1563).

The Reformation and westward expansion

After German-speaking Switzerland, the Reformation spread to the French-speaking regions.

Vaud, Neuchâtel and Geneva became Protestant. Geneva even became a centre of the Reformation. Bern conquered Vaud. Fribourg and Valais expanded their territory.

In the west, Switzerland reached approximately its present frontiers.

In Geneva, those seeking the independence of the city counted on the support of the Confederates, or "Eidgenossen" in German. The German word was difficult to pronounce in French and became "Eyguenots," which may have been the origin of the term "Huguenot" used later to refer to all French Calvinists.

DO YOU HAVE ANYTHING MORE SEVERE?

The work of Farel and Viret

- Held back in German-speaking cantons after the defeat at Kappel, the Reformation spread westward.

- From 1526, Guillaume Farel, a French priest employed by Bern, preached sermons in favour of the Reformation. After converting Aigle, a Bernese possession, he continued in Morat, Grandson and Orbe, where Pierre Viret became his disciple. He then brought the county of Neuchâtel and finally Geneva into his camp.

- During a public debate in Lausanne in 1536 (known as the "Dispute of Lausanne"), Farel, Viret and Calvin won their case against the Catholics, despite the latter having a substantial numerical majority; thus the Reformation was established in Vaud.

The Protestant Rome

- After the flight of its bishop in 1533, Geneva became a free Republic. With the help of Viret, Farel succeeded in abolishing Catholic religious services in the town in 1535; Geneva adopted the Reformation on 21 May 1536.

- Farel then called on the help of Jean Calvin, a French reformer who had sought refuge in Basel. The new arrival, however, met with strong opposition and was expelled from Geneva from 1538 to 1541. On his return, he established theocratic rule – government by the Church.

Under Church government, everything that was considered contrary to moral principles was repressed. Theatre, games, dancing, certain clothes and hair styling were forbidden. Adversaries of the government were executed. One such was the Spanish doctor and theologian Michel Servet, burned alive in 1553 for heresy (opinion contrary to Church doctrine).

- The radical ideas of Jean Calvin were influential in Switzerland and Protestant Europe. Geneva was known as the "Protestant Rome."

As in Lausanne in 1537, the Reformation led, in 1559, to the establishment in Geneva of an Academy (predecessor of the University) to train clergy. Theodore of Bèze (Calvin's successor) became the rector. Foreign students came to Geneva to study there.

The conquest of Vaud

- The western frontiers of Switzerland took shape. Until 1536, the Duchy of Savoy possessed the majority of Vaud, the Geneva region and lower Valais. Lausanne and Geneva were autonomous bishoprics under the Holy Roman Empire. Morat, Grandson, Orbe and Echallens were joint possessions of Bern and Fribourg.

- The Duke of Savoy wanted to take the town of Geneva, but their allies, the **Bernese**, sent their army against him. On the way, between January and March 1536, Bern conquered Vaud.

- Once in Geneva, which managed to retain its independence, the Bernese, having overcome the Savoy forces, conquered Gex and part of the southern shore of the Lac Léman (region around Evian). They were forced to return these lands to Savoy in 1567.

- Bern finished its conquest of Vaud by taking over Lausanne, where the Reformation was implemented; as in Geneva, the bishop fled.

Fribourg and Valais on the attack

- In 1536-37, Fribourg, which was also seeking expansion, grabbed the territory formerly controlled by Savoy between Estavayer-le-Lac and Châtel-Saint-Denis.

In 1554, crippled by debts, the Count of Gruyère was forced to cede his lands to Fribourg and Bern; Fribourg's frontiers came close to where they are today.

- The forces of Valais invaded the Chablais (Monthey) and pressed as far as Thonon, on the southern shore of Lac Léman. In 1569, however, they had to return to Savoy all territory beyond St. Gingolph.

- From 1537, the Confederation controlled almost all of French-speaking Switzerland, within boundaries similar to those of today.

During their conquest of Vaud, the Bernese took the Chateau of Chillon, near Villeneuve (VD) and released François Bonivard of Geneva, imprisoned there for his opposition to Savoy; thanks to the poem *The Prisoner of Chillon* by the early 19th century English poet, Lord Byron, a leading figure in Romanticism, Bonivard subsequently became a hero.

The Ancien Régime

For three centuries Switzer-land was made up of various separate territories, including the thirteen cantons, each with a different constitutional status.

Despite an appearance of democracy, most power was concentrated in the hands of rich and powerful families (this is what was known as the Ancien Régime*). The Confederation was totally decentralised and the Diet was powerless.*

This system only changed with the revolutions at the end of the 18th century.

Swiss territory (⋯⋗ Map 4, p. 39)

- Under the *Ancien Régime*, Switzerland comprised:
  - five rural cantons: UR, SZ, NW/OW, GL, AI/AR;
  - seven town cantons (towns and dependent territories): LU, ZH, BE, FR, SO, BA*, SH;
  - one mixed canton: ZG;
  - regions under joint rule (territory belonging to several cantons – from two to twelve in some cases – and administered by each of them in turn during successive periods);

    Joint rule: Echallens, Grandson, Orbe; Mex, Morat, Schwarzenburg, Baden, Freie Aemter (in present-day Aargau - "Free Bailiwicks" in English), Thurgau, Rheintal, Uznach, Gaster, Gams, Sargans, Valmaggia, Locarno, Lugano, Mendrisio.

  - allies (territories linked to the Confederation without being members, together with their dependent lands).

    Allies: Valais; Graubünden and their jointly controlled territory of Valtellina; the towns of Biel-Bienne, Mulhouse, St. Gallen and Rottweil; the county of Neuchâtel; the abbey of St. Gallen; the town and republic of Geneva; the bishopric of Basel; the abbey of Engelberg; the republic of Gersau.

Uncertain frontiers

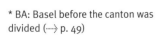

- Some allies had links with only a few of the cantons.

  For example: Neuchâtel was allied only with Bern and Solothurn. When the ruling family died out in 1707, Neuchâtel became Prussian (Prussia was a kingdom in northern Germany), but remained allied to the Confederation.

- Some territories were only partially allied.

  For example: the French-speaking part of the bishopric of Basel (today the canton of Jura) was much closer to the Confederation than the German-speaking part (Laufen), which retained very close links to the Holy Roman Empire.

- The limits of the Confederation of thirteen cantons – not always well-defined – were close to the present-day frontiers.

  The allied town of Mulhouse (Alsace) as well as Valtellina (south of Graubünden) are no longer part of Switzerland. On the other hand, several communes of Geneva, together with the Fricktal (north of Aargau) and the feudal territory of Tarasp (east of Graubünden), were then not yet part of the country.

* BA: Basel before the canton was divided (⋯⋗ p. 49)

A frozen system

- After 1536, the Swiss abandoned their military ambitions and moved more and more in the direction of neutrality (despite the continuation of the alliance with France, which was concluded under the 1516 peace agreement after the battle of Marignano ⋯⋗ p. 27). By signing several agreements with the surrounding powers, they allowed their men to fight in large numbers as mercenaries for foreign sovereigns.

  Up to 60,000 Swiss mercenaries were engaged outside the country at the same time.

- Up to 1798, despite differences of opinion on religion and town/country issues, the structure of the Confederation changed little.

  At the time, Switzerland was known as "the Helvetic Body" ("corps helvétique"), the "Thirteen Cantons" or "the Leagues." The only common institution was the Diet (⋯⋗ p. 26), the members of which could not be forced to implement its decisions.

- Power was concentrated in the hands of a few rich, essentially urban, families. The system of government was to all appearances democratic, but its renewal was decided between bourgeois or aristocratic members of society. Despite the old principle of equality between free men, the inhabitants were subjects (i.e. they had no rights). The trade corporations were very influential.

  In the canton of Vaud, one can still read on some buildings the inscription "LLEE" which stands for "Leurs Excellences de Berne" ("Their Excellencies of Bern"). This refers to the governing class of Bern that occupied Vaud at this time.

In the night of 11/12 December 1602, a Savoy army numbering 2000 attempted to take Geneva by climbing the ramparts. Part of the invading force managed to enter the town, but the inhabitants reacted quickly and expelled or captured them. This resistance was symbolised by the action of Catherine Royaume (known as "Mère Royaume") who, according to legend, dropped a cauldron of soup on the head of a Savoy soldier climbing the walls. At the beginning of December, the people of Geneva still commemorate the "Escalade" and "Mère Royaume" by breaking cooking pots made of chocolate.

1616-1798
Full independence

At the end of the Thirty Years' War, the Peace of Westphalia granted Switzerland independence.

The Confederation confirmed its neutrality. Apart from a few minor conflicts, the country enjoyed peace and a degree of prosperity.

In some upper strata of society, the notion of belonging to a Swiss "nation" took root.

The Peace of Westphalia (1648)

- From 1618 to 1648, the **Thirty Years' War** spread destruction across Europe. The Holy Roman Empire and its Catholic allies fought against the other European powers, most of which were Protestant. Despite links between each religious group and foreign powers, the Confederates overcame their differences. Switzerland started on the path towards **armed neutrality**: not getting involved in conflicts but defending itself if attacked. In response to foreign incursions in 1633 and 1638, the Diet raised an army of 36,000 men.

  Only the Grey Leagues (Graubünden) were affected by the Thirty Years' War.

- Whenever the Confederation was threatened, a War Council was called. In 1647, after French and Swedish attacks in Thurgau, the Council promulgated a pact for territorial defence known as the "Defensionale of Wil."

  In 1673, a new defensive pact was signed between the thirteen cantons and four of their allies. It was more binding than its predecessor and was the first formal national agreement on military cooperation.

- In 1648, the Peace of Westphalia (a region in the north-west of Germany) put an end to the Thirty Years' War. Johann Rudolf Wettstein of Basel, negotiating on behalf of the Confederation, obtained recognition by the whole of Europe of Switzerland's **full independence**.

  The Holy Roman Empire gave up control of Basel, Appenzell, Schaffhausen and St. Gallen.

WHAT DOES ARMED NEUTRALITY MEAN?

KEEP SWISS KNIVES CLOSED!

Internal unrest

- The Confederation suffered some internal conflicts during this period: in 1653, the peasants revolted against their harsh living conditions. The cantons got together to crush this "Peasants' War" within a few months.

- Two religious wars were fought at Villmergen (AG). The Catholics won the first in 1656, but lost the second in 1712. The subsequent Peace of Aarau established the equality of the two religions and freedom of choice of confession.

The 18th century

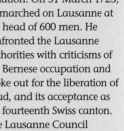

- At this time Switzerland was a fairly peaceful and prosperous Confederation, counting some 1.5 million inhabitants. Its economy was one of the most flourishing in Europe. The know-how and expertise of the Protestants who fled from France to settle in Switzerland (the Huguenots) contributed to this prosperity. Many came to Basel, bringing the skills of the textile industry with them.

- **Agriculture** developed. Land use was improved and new crops were introduced (e.g. potato, tobacco). Agricultural produce became important commercially. However, the peasants received little benefit and had to find additional resources to survive. As a result, they became an important source of labour (frequently as "cottage industry" with tools provided to them) for two sectors in full expansion: watchmaking (in Geneva and then the Jura arc) and textiles (especially in Zurich).

- **Mercenary** service remained an important source of income (in 1701, there were 54,000 men under arms abroad) – and because the Confederation could call them up when needed, the European powers who employed them left Switzerland in peace.

- In 1761, a group of intellectuals set up the "Helvetic Association" with the aim of furthering the idea of a Swiss "nation," in which each person would work for the common good. Switzerland excelled in the **sciences**, thanks, in particular, to Leonhard Euler, the mathematician from Basel, and Horace Bénédict de Saussure, the Geneva scientist.

- The beauty of the alpine landscapes and the Swiss libertarian tradition attracted foreign travellers (wealthy English, in particular), marking the start of **tourism** in Switzerland.

The inhabitants of Vaud, who had been under Bernese domination since 1536, had no political rights. Major **Jean-Daniel Abraham Davel**, decided to remedy this situation. On 31 March 1723, he marched on Lausanne at the head of 600 men. He confronted the Lausanne authorities with criticisms of the Bernese occupation and spoke out for the liberation of Vaud, and its acceptance as the fourteenth Swiss canton. The Lausanne Council warned the Bernese, who captured Davel and beheaded him in Vidy. At the time, this act of revolt passed almost unnoticed. It was only in the 19th century that Davel was recognised as the first patriot of Vaud.

1291-1798

The growth of Swiss territory

Within a few centuries, the Confederation evolved from a small number of alpine valleys to a country with frontiers similar to those of today.

1. The "original" Switzerland, 1291

┈┈> p. 21

2. The Confederation of eight cantons, 1388

┈┈> p. 22

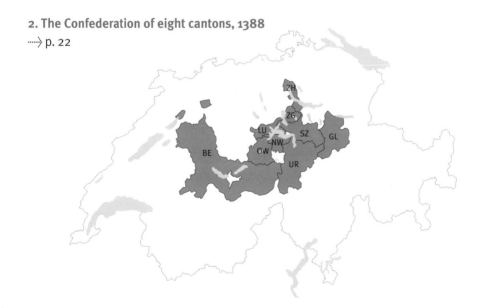

3. The Confederation of thirteen cantons, 1513

⤙⤙⤙⤑ p. 26

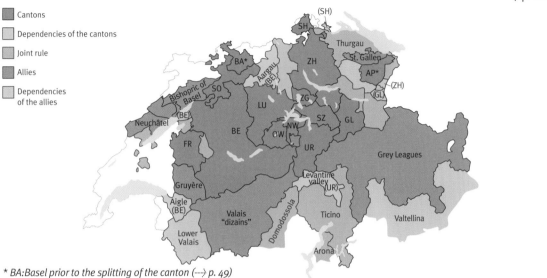

Cantons
Dependencies of the cantons
Joint rule
Allies
Dependencies of the allies

* BA: Basel prior to the splitting of the canton (⤙⤙⤙⤑ p. 49)
  AP: Appenzell prior to the splitting of the canton (⤙⤙⤙⤑ p. 31)

4. Switzerland under the *Ancien Régime*, 1536-1798

⤙⤙⤙⤑ p. 34

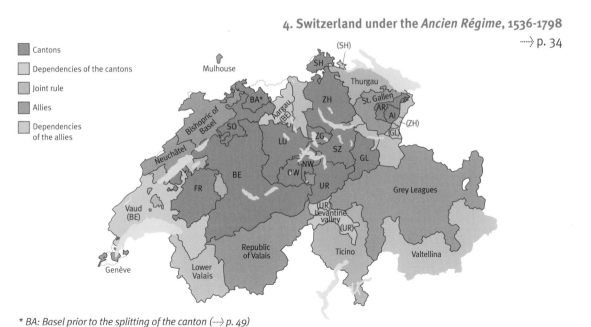

Cantons
Dependencies of the cantons
Joint rule
Allies
Dependencies of the allies

* BA: Basel prior to the splitting of the canton (⤙⤙⤙⤑ p. 49)

Transition to modern Switzerland

(1798-1847)

1789-1798

Revolution in Switzerland

The French Revolution led to the collapse of the Confederation.

In several towns and cantons, the aristocratic regimes were overthrown. France invaded Switzerland, which was too weak and divided to resist.

Switzerland became a satellite of revolutionary France and then of Napoleon.

Echoes from Paris

• In 1789, what became known as The French Revolution broke out in Paris. It lasted a decade and brought about the fall of the monarchy.

• Events in Paris soon found echoes in the Swiss cantons. Patriotic ideas and **demands for democracy** spread, particularly among the intellectual and business elites. However, the cantonal authorities, in the hands of a few privileged families, refused any idea of reform and suppressed all attempts at change.

From 1790, the bishopric of Basel, lower Valais, Vaud, Valtellina, Zurich and St. Gallen were particularly affected by popular demonstrations.

• Those Swiss who supported the Revolution found refuge in Paris, where they founded a "Helvetic Club," whose influence was limited, since it was active only from 1790 to 1791.

In 1792, Bern and Zurich sent their troops to Geneva to prevent a French invasion. An agreement was reached between the two sides and both withdrew. The revolutionaries nevertheless seized power a few weeks later, and it was in Geneva that the Revolution enjoyed its first Swiss success.

• Events in Paris were reflected in the newly created Swiss press. A high point of emotion was reached with the news of the massacre of the Swiss Guards on 10 August 1792. They were defending the Tuileries Palace, under attack by the mob who were trying to capture Louis XVI. Further massacres took place in September. In all, 5000 Swiss died during this unrest.

In Lucerne, a statue of a dying lion was erected in 1823 in memory of the Swiss killed in Paris.

The French invasion

- Revolutionary France sought protection against the other European powers and surrounded itself with buffer States. It put Switzerland under pressure with the aim of gaining control of the mountain passes and seizing Swiss wealth. Given the divisions between its members, the Confederation began to collapse under this threat.

THE FRENCH INVADED SWITZERLAND…

…TWO HUNDRED YEARS BEFORE WORK PERMITS!

- In 1792, France invaded the north of the Basel bishopric and declared a Republic. However, after only a few months, France simply took over the territory (present-day Jura canton).

Five years later, the south of the bishopric was invaded. Basel granted freedom and equality to all its subjects.

- In 1795, **Frédéric César de la Harpe**, from Vaud, called on the people of Vaud to rise against the aristocrats of Bern; his appeal fell on deaf ears and he fled to Paris, where he encouraged the French government to send troops.

- In 1797, the Confederation lost Valtellina to the new Cisalpine Republic, a French client state in northern Italy. At the end of the year, **Napoleon Bonaparte** pressed the French government to invade and "liberate" Switzerland; 10,000 men arrived near Geneva.

- At the beginning of 1798, everything speeded up. The urban elites of Vaud (if not the population, which got on quite well under the Bernese occupation) proclaimed the Lemanic Republic at Lausanne. A few days later, a French general – under the pretext that two of his soldiers had been killed at Thierrens (VD) – invaded Switzerland. Bern did not react. A month later, the towns, the cantons and their allies were in active revolt. Within a few weeks, more than forty Republics had been declared, all destined to be short-lived.

- This episode marked the end of the *Ancien Régime* in Switzerland. The Bernese had to capitulate after their defeat at Grauholz (north of Bern). Between the spring and autumn of 1798, a few regions – including central Switzerland – rose against the French but were violently suppressed. Nidwalden was sacked.

At the end of 1798, just after the violent suppression of the anti-French demonstrations in Nidwalden, the Helvetic Republic (⋯⟶ p. 44) sent Henri Pestalozzi, already a famous teacher, to Stans, the main town, to collect and take care of the war orphans. At his institution in Yverdon (VD), he applied his concepts of childhood education based on teacher-pupil sympathy. He is considered a pioneer of modern educational theory.

1798-1813

The Republic and the Act of Mediation

France occupied Switzerland and gave the country new political institutions.

In contrast to the Confederal system, the Helvetic Republic envisaged full centralisation – it was not, however, implemented. Napoleon authorised a partial return to the Ancien Régime.

A vassal of France, Switzerland enjoyed a few years of peace and the beginnings of democracy.

After the collapse of the Confederation on 5 March 1798, Switzerland was nearly split into pieces. France planned three client States: the *Rhodanic Republic* (Vaud, Fribourg, Bernese Oberland, Valais, Ticino); *Tellgovia* (*Tellgau* in German – central Switzerland and Graubünden); and the *Helvetic Republic* (the rest of the country). The plan was never put into effect.

Helvetic Republic (┈┊ map 5, p. 47)

- In March 1798, republican France imposed on Switzerland a State system based on its own: the "Helvetic Republic, one and indivisible" (the official name). It was a **unitary and centralised State**, the very opposite of the Confederal tradition.

- Peter Ochs of Basel drafted a constitution in Paris that provided for:
  – two legislative councils that were to elect an executive entity ("directoire") of five members, with headquarters in Aarau;
  – abolition of feudal rights (which took a long time to disappear);
  – introduction of certain freedoms (opinion, press, property) – not always implemented.

- The cantons became simply administrative entities under the governorship of a "Prefect." Frontiers were subject to many alterations.

  For example: the Jura and Geneva were part of France; the small cantons of central Switzerland were brought together in a single canton "Waldstätten."

An impossible arrangement

- The French liberating force became a detested occupying power. The taxes levied on Switzerland were heavy. Society was torn between "Unitarians" (favouring new ideas and a centralised power) and "Federalists" (preferring the return of the *Ancien Régime*). The coffers were empty and everything had to be set up from scratch (administration, education, etc.).

- **Instability** was rife. There were several *coups d'état*. Neutrality was forcibly replaced by a military alliance with France. In 1799-1800, the warring European powers also fought on Swiss soil.

- Napoleon became First Consul in 1799. He withdrew his troops from Switzerland in 1802, but continued to govern the country, which veered into chaos. Exiled to Lausanne, the government controlled almost nothing.

The Act of Mediation (⋯⟩ Map 6, p. 47)

- On 30 September 1802, **Napoleon** forcibly mediated between the Swiss and called an Assembly of 63 representatives of the "Unitarians" and the "Federalists" in Paris. The **Act of Mediation** was announced on 19 February 1803: Switzerland was given new institutions.

- The central power was vested in a single Assembly ("Diet"), to meet once a year by rotation in six "major" cantons ("cantons directeurs" – FR, BE, SO, BA*, ZH, LU). The highest officer in the host canton became the "Landammann" (Chief Magistrate) of Switzerland: he ruled the country for the subsequent period.

  The "Mediation" was the only time in Swiss history when a single person ruled the land.

- Switzerland had **nineteen cantons,** each of which had its own constitution. The rural cantons reintroduced the popular assembly ("Landsgemeinde"), a form of direct democracy with voting by show of hands, that had been practised in central Switzerland since the 13th century. The towns reverted to an aristocratic and corporative system, but more moderate than that prior to 1798. There were six new cantons (⋯⟩ p. 46), formerly allied territories, subjects or regions under joint rule, whose institutions were partially democratic.

- Prior to 1798, there had been customs duties between cantons – these were not reintroduced, but road tolls remained. Officially there was only one currency, the Franc, but in practice the cantons retained their monetary systems. The Federal army was made up of cantonal contingents.

- Although under French control – and sometimes threatened with annexation – Switzerland enjoyed ten years of peace (1803-1813). However, industry (especially textiles) suffered from the embargo imposed by the enemies of Napoleon, who had crowned himself emperor in 1804.

* *Basel prior to the split of the canton (⋯⟩ p. 49)*

Masters of Switzerland since 1798, the French pillaged the land and enriched themselves – making possible Napoleon's campaign in Egypt. They also acquired an important pool of manpower that was forced to fight for the empire. At least 30,000 Swiss served under Napoleon between 1798 and 1815. Some gave their lives for him; in 1812, the battle of Berezina alone (at which France fought the Russians) led to more than 7000 deaths among the Swiss: however, many Swiss under French arms died from illness (cholera) without even having fought.

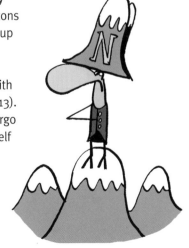

From thirteen to twenty-two cantons

In less than twenty years, Switzerland's frontiers changed several times.

Powerless during the Helvetic Republic, the cantons regained their sovereignty – first under the Act of Mediation, then under the Federal Pact.

Switzerland acquired its present frontiers.

Nine new members

Nine new cantons joined the Confederation in two waves: 1803 and 1815.

 Aargau, 1803 – Formerly a Habsburg territory – partly conquered by the Confederation, then divided up between Austria, Bern and other joint rulers – Aargau was divided in two in 1798 before becoming a canton.

AG

 Graubünden, 1803 – Graubünden was a confederation of federal states, allied to the Swiss Confederation, and became a canton. In 1815, they unsuccessfully sought to regain their independence.

GR

 St. Gallen, 1803 – for centuries, two sources of power had co-existed in St. Gallen: the Abbey and the town – and both had been allied to different cantons. In 1803, their various lands, subject territories and regions under joint rule were united.

SG

Ticino, 1803 – Northern Ticino (Levantine valley) was under the rule of Uri and the south was sub-divided under various forms of joint rule before a united canton emerged.

TI

 Thurgau, 1803 – This former Habsburg territory was conquered by the Confederation in the 15th century and fell under joint rule before becoming a canton.

TG

 Vaud, 1803 – First belonging to Savoy and then Bern (1536), Vaud comprised four territories under joint rule under the *Ancien Régime*. After a revolution of the middle classes in 1798, the whole area of Vaud became a canton in 1803.

VD

 Geneva, 1815 – In 1533 the burghers of Geneva took complete control of the city from the bishop. Under French domination from 1798 to 1815, Geneva then became a canton, incorporating at the same time several neighbouring communities.

GE

Neuchâtel, 1815 – The principality of Neuchâtel had been controlled by Prussia since 1707. It became a canton, retaining simultaneously its status as a Prussian principality until 1857 (⋯⋙ p. 58).

NE

 Valais, 1815 – During the *Ancien Régime*, upper and central Valais had been a Republic, of which lower Valais was a dependent subject. Gaining its independence in 1803, it became a canton after a short period under French control (1810-1815).

VS

Swiss territory from 1798 to 1815

5. Helvetic Republic, 1798
⋯⟩ p. 44

6. Act of Mediation, 1803
⋯⟩ p. 45

7. Federal Pact, 1815
⋯⟩ p. 48

** BA: Basel prior to the splitting of
the canton (⋯⟩ p. 49)*

Restoration and Regeneration

The fall of Napoleon ended French control of Switzerland.

The Federal Pact of 1815 brought about an almost total reversion to the Ancien Régime *(political system prior to the French Revolution) – known as the "Restoration." Around 1830, the cantons moved progressively towards democracy – known as the "Regeneration."*

Liberals attempted to promote their ideas: centralisation of the State combined with individual liberties.

In 1815, after the battle of Waterloo (defeat of Napoleon), the 24,000-strong Federal army marched into the Franche-Comté and Gex. For a few months, it occupied these frontier regions. This was the last time that Swiss armed forces intervened abroad (until peace-making missions in the 20ᵗʰ century).

The Federal Pact

- In December 1813, the armies of the coalition against Napoleon (Austria, Prussia and Russia) crossed Switzerland to attack France. The Diet and army could do nothing. This was the end of French domination of Switzerland and thus of the "mediation."

Several cantons, including Bern, took advantage of the situation to restore the Ancien Régime. A Republic was proclaimed in Biel-Bienne and Geneva (both of which had been annexed by France).

- The cantons were divided. At the beginning of 1814, there were two competing Diets: one for the conservative cantons (in favour of the *Ancien Régime*), the other for the progressive cantons (influenced by liberal ideas). The continued existence of the six new cantons from 1803 appeared to be threatened: Bern, for example, attempted to take back Aargau. However, an agreement was reached between all the cantons and a "Federal Pact" was concluded on 7 August 1815. The **"Swiss Confederation"** (today still the official name of Switzerland) was constituted, made up of independent cantons.

The Diet (central political institution of the new Confederation) only had power in foreign policy. It met by rotation in one of the main cantons (ZH, BE, LU). The cantons were responsible for manning and equipping a Federal army.

Switzerland at the Congress of Vienna

- After the defeat of Napoleon, a Congress was held in Vienna from 1814 to 1815 to reorganise Europe. The victorious powers sought to protect themselves by surrounding France with buffer States, including Switzerland.

- The Treaty of Paris was signed at the conclusion of the Congress of Vienna in 1815. In it, the allies gave formal recognition of the **"inviolability of Switzerland"** and its **"perpetual neutrality."** Switzerland acquired its present frontiers.

Three new cantons joined the Confederation (⤳ p. 46). Bern was granted the former bishopric of Basel (Jura, Bernese Jura and Laufen) in compensation for the cession of territory that went to the new canton of Aargau.

CONGRESS OF VIENNA

THE NEGOTIATIONS WERE A PIECE OF CAKE!

Return to the *Ancien Régime*

- In France, the **Restoration** marked the return to monarchy in 1814-1815. Switzerland experienced a similar return to pre-Revolutionary ways and the *Ancien Régime*: limited personal freedoms, power held by the aristocracy and the corporations.

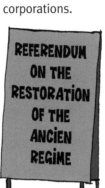

- The new cantons, like Vaud, were relatively progressive (supportive of liberal ideas promoting democracy and defending individual liberties). However, they were called to order by the old cantons.

  For example, in Vaud only the richest citizens had the right to vote.

- Switzerland gave refuge to foreign dissidents. The conservative European powers kept careful watch on the country.

- At this time, economic development moved ahead, but was slowed by cantonal trade barriers. There were customs posts between the cantons, only twelve had a standardised system of weights and measures and the single currency introduced at the time of the Act of Mediation disappeared.

A touch of democracy

- In Switzerland, the **Regeneration** is the period during which, following the 1830 revolution in France, liberal ideas moved forward. Equality of rights and the vote for all were demanded.

- Influenced by these ideas, half the cantons (including BE, ZH, VD and FR) gradually liberalised their constitutions. Liberals came to power.

  In 1832, the liberals put forward a proposal in the Diet for revising the Federal Pact to guarantee more individual freedom, but it was refused.

- Elsewhere (especially in Neuchâtel and central Switzerland), the Regeneration failed. In **1832**, after a civil war, the town of **Basel** (conservative) and the surrounding countryside (more progressive) split into two separate half-cantons: Basel Town (BS) and Basel Country (BL).

In 1832, after the failure in the Diet of the attempt to revise the Federal Pact, the only reform implemented was to fix the date of the Federal day of fasting on the third Sunday of September. This idea had been put forward in 1794 by the canton of Bern with the aim of strengthening the Confederation against revolutionary movements. This celebration brought together Catholics and Protestants in the medieval tradition of days of penitence. Only Geneva did not follow suit and kept its own day of fasting, the "Jeûne Genevois."

1815-1847

The Sonderbund *war*

Excessive decentralisation hampered the development of the Confederation and there was no consensus on the way ahead.

Religious tensions set fire to the powder keg. Seven cantons seceded. A civil war broke out but it was short and caused few casualties.

The radicals – who promoted democracy and the centralisation of the country – came out of the conflict as the victors.

A divided Switzerland

- From 1815, Swiss politics comprised two opposing factions. The conservative one insisted on the independence of the cantons. The liberal one claimed a more centralised State and more democracy. On top of this, there were also other forms of opposition: Catholics against Protestants, countryside against town, elites against the people.

  Contemporary observers wrote of "anarchy" or "chaos." They feared the dissolution of the Confederation. Despite these tensions, the idea of Switzerland as a common fatherland gained ground in people's minds during the first half of the 19ᵗʰ century.

- There was not much industrialisation and peasants were in the majority. Poor harvests and rising prices caused poverty and insecurity. From 1845 to 1847, potato blight caused the last famine in Switzerland.

  One fifth of the 200,000 population of Vaud lived in poverty.

- Further left than the liberals, the radicals wanted to change the system by introducing democracy and centralising power. For their opponents they were revolutionaries.

Monasteries, convents and the Jesuits

Two crises led to civil war in Switzerland.

- Following a Catholic peasant revolt, the canton of Aargau – governed by a radical – decided in 1841 to close the monasteries and convents, in contravention of the Federal Pact. The Diet negotiated a compromise, allowing the convents to be reopened (but not the monasteries).

- The conservative Catholic cantons tried to limit the influence of the liberals. In 1845, Lucerne entrusted the education of priests to the Jesuits. The radicals, convinced that the brotherhood was in league with the conservatives, were scandalised. In the Diet, liberals and radicals narrowly came short of a majority for expelling the Jesuits.

Towards war

- In September 1843, six conservative Catholic cantons (UR, SZ, NW/OW, LU, ZG, FR) concluded a **secret defensive military alliance** (revealed in 1846). Later, their opponents would call this the "Sonderbund," meaning "special alliance." Valais joined the Catholic allies in 1844; Neuchâtel and Appenzell/Innerrhoden, despite their conservative leanings, remained neutral.

  The Federal Pact authorised agreements between cantons, but not with foreign entities. Nevertheless, the seven cantons of the Sonderbund *negotiated the support of several countries; France and Prussia even sent troops to the Swiss frontier.*

- The radicals, after taking power by force in Vaud and Geneva and winning the elections in St. Gallen, held a majority in the Diet, which voted the dissolution of the *Sonderbund* on 20 July 1847. There was no way to avoid **civil war**.

If they had been victorious, some leaders of the *Sonderbund* intended to alter the map of Switzerland to the benefit of the Catholics. Constantin Siegwart-Müller of Lucerne planned the creation of a canton of the Jura. All of northern Vaud would have gone to Fribourg and the eastern part, from Vevey onwards, to Valais. Fribourg would have also gained part of the Bernese Oberland and the Simmental; Valais and Obwalden would have shared what was left of the Oberland. The whole of Catholic Aargau, together with Zofingen and Aarburg would have gone to Lucerne. Glarus would have been divided between Schwyz and Uri. Zug would have expanded northwards at Zurich's expense.

Three weeks of war

- In November 1847, the Federal army (comprising 100,000 men commanded by **General Guillaume-Henri Dufour**) clashed with the 80,000 soldiers of the *Sonderbund*, under the command of General Johann Ulrich von Salis-Soglio.

  It was paradoxical that the radical and progressive camp was led by a conservative (Dufour) and that the Catholic separatists were led by a Protestant (von Salis-Soglio).

- In large part thanks to the skill and pragmatism of General Dufour, the Federal army emerged victorious from the *Sonderbund* war after only three weeks. Fribourg was first to fall. Uri tried in vain to attack Ticino. Zug capitulated without fighting.

- The main attack was directed against the canton of Lucerne at Gislikon (LU) on 23 November 1847, when the Federal army obtained a decisive victory. In the following days the remaining separatist cantons laid down their arms and their leaders fled to Italy. The human cost of the *Sonderbund* war was about a hundred dead and three hundred wounded.

The establishment of the Federal State (1848-1914)

1848

The first Federal Constitution

After the Sonderbund war, Switzerland acquired new institutions.

It became a Federal State, comprising sovereign cantons. The country was governed by a seven-member Council and a two-tier parliament. The Confederation acquired new centralised powers.

The political system put in place in 1848 is still in force today.

For the drafting of the Federal Constitution, the Diet called on the radical members of cantonal governments. The freshly constituted Federal parliament elected most of the original members of the first Federal Council on 16 November 1848. The first President of the Confederation was Jonas Furrer of Zurich.

SIRE, SWITZERLAND IS SUFFERING FROM DEMOCRATIC FEVER!

Post-war

- In the aftermath of the *Sonderbund* war, the Federal army occupied the seven Catholic cantons that had been at the origin of the conflict – their conservative governments were overthrown. The costs of the war were onerous. They were imposed on the Catholic and the neutral cantons.

- The victory of the progressive camp was so rapid that the conservative powers (France, Austria and Prussia) had no time to intervene. They attempted to check the democratic aims of the radicals – but, beginning in Paris in February 1848, revolutions broke out in Europe and kept them fully occupied.

Switzerland was a pioneer, initiating (and successfully achieving) a transition to democracy ahead of the rest of Europe.

The revision of the Federal Pact

- The Diet (in which the radicals held the majority) set out to remodel the institutions of State. It approved a draft Constitution and then submitted it for ratification to the cantons, where it passed with a majority of fifteen and a half against six and a half. The **Constitution** was proclaimed on 12 September 1848.

The six and a half cantons that rejected the Constitution were: UR, SZ, ZG, VS, TI, NW/OW, AI.

- Switzerland became a **centralised Federal State**, but continued to call itself a "Confederation." The cantons were no longer independent but "sovereign" (i.e. autonomous). They handed over some of their powers to the Confederation.

A Confederation is an alliance between independent States. A Federation has a central government to which the most important functions have been delegated.

- A democratic system was put in place. Citizens acquired rights and freedoms and were considered equal before the law. However, women did not have the vote.

The Constitution of 1848 guaranteed: the right to choose their place of residence for citizens professing the Christian faith; freedom to practice Christian rites (however, the Jesuits were banned); freedom of the press; freedom of association, meetings and petitions; freedom to engage in trade and industry.

The new institutions

- The Federal Council (government) was set up, with seven members and a rotating one-year Presidency (President of the Confederation). It is the executive power.

- The **Federal Parliament** is the legislative power. It comprises two Houses, one representing the people (National Council), the other representing the cantons (Council of States). The former separatist (Catholic) cantons, thinly populated, have little weight in the National Council; but in the Council of States they have the same number of representatives as the other cantons.

  The National Council was originally elected for three years, with one seat per 20,000 inhabitants, making a total of 111. The Council of States was also elected for three years and comprised two seats per canton (one per half-canton), making a total of 44.

A centralised State

- Until 1848, the Confederation was concerned only with foreign affairs. The new Constitution gave it new centralised powers:
  - elimination of customs barriers between the cantons and establishment of common external tariffs;

    Customs revenues were the main financial resource of the Confederation; taxes were levied by the cantons for their own benefit.
  - single postal system with identical stamps and rates;
  - centralised army;
  - **single currency:** the French denomination, Franc, was chosen over the Central European Florin;
  - standardised weights and measures: the foot, the pound and the pot.

    The present decimal system (metres and grams) was the choice of the French-speaking cantons, but was not adopted until 1868 and came into force in 1874.

- These various measures promoted general **prosperity**, one of the objectives of the Constitution. Common institutions and administration simplified economic development.

- The cantons retained their autonomy in education, health, roads, public works, judiciary and religion. Each had its own Constitution, government (State Council/Conseil d'Etat/Regierungs- or Staatsrat), Parliament (Grand Council/Grand Conseil/Kantons- or Grosser Rat), laws, administration, police and finances (taxes were levied by the cantons).

At its first session in November 1848, Parliament had to decide where to locate the central institutions. Bern, Zurich and Lucerne were the candidates; Aarau (AG) and Zofingen (AG) had also been considered. Some people wanted to build a new Federal city, following the example of Washington D.C. Finally, Bern was chosen (with the support of the French-speaking cantons). The first administrative and legislative headquarters (the Federal "Palace") was completed in 1857 – the west wing of the present building dates from 1902. In compensation, Zurich received the Technical University (ETH) in 1854.

MID-19th CENTURY: STANDARDISED CURRENCY

END-20th CENTURY: STANDARDISED THINKING!

The Constitution of 1874

The wounds of the civil war took time to heal. Discord remained.

Gradually, some cantons extended people's rights. In 1874, the revised Constitution introduced the optional referendum and strengthened central power at the expense of the cantons.

The 1874 Constitution remained in force until the end of the 20th century.

IT'S VERY IMPORTANT THAT WE ALL PULL TOGETHER...

...AND DON'T GO SHOOTING OFF IN DIFFERENT DIRECTIONS!

SHOOTING PRACTICE

General Dufour, who commanded the Federal army during the *Sonderbund* war, became an icon of national reconciliation. So-called *Dufourli,* tobacco pipes carved in his effigy, sold like hot cakes in central Switzerland. Dufour was also a topographer. He was responsible for the "Dufour map," the first accurate geographic representation of Switzerland (1864).

Continued dissension

• Despite the peace and the creation of new institutions, post-1848 Switzerland was still torn with dissension. The defeated former Sonderbund cantons were still licking their wounds. There was real hatred between the central cantons and the cantons on the Plateau.

• In the first federal elections in November 1848, the **Radicals** obtained an overwhelming majority. Despite the split in their ranks between a left wing favouring a more centralised State, and a right wing with liberal leanings, especially in relation to the economy, they gained power in a majority of cantons.

   • Radical reforms came up against old traditions. The separation of Church and State, laid down in cantonal constitutions, was not to the liking of the Pope and to some Swiss Catholics; this is what was known as the "culture war" *(Kulturkampf).*

   • From 1848, the defeated and neutral cantons paid war reparations to the Confederation. In 1852, debts under this heading were cancelled, which led to a slight improvement in relations.

Opposition to the radicals

• The **Conservatives** became stronger and sometimes regained power, as in Lucerne in 1871.

• The Radical leaders had a monopoly of power in the economy and politics: they were the bourgeois camp. A mixed group opposed them: a nascent labour movement, peasants clinging to their traditions, artisans in financial difficulty, democratic intellectuals, the former aristocracy. These varied opposition groups succeeded in finding common cause in agitating for further popular rights and in trying to get back into power.

An anti-radical alliance governed in Vaud between 1861 and 1866. In Geneva a struggle pitted a similar coalition against James Fazy's Radicals. The Conservatives (in alliance with the Liberals) regained power in Fribourg in 1857.

Redrafting the Constitution

- Political discord opened the way to a redrafting of the Federal Constitution with the aim of giving Bern additional central powers, increasing popular rights and secularising the State.

- The revision to the Constitution was incorporated in the 1848 text but required what is known as a "double majority" – i.e. of cantons and total votes. In 1872, a first draft was rejected as pushing centralisation too far. In 1874, a consensus was reached with the dropping of the unification of laws: the cantons retained their own civil and penal law – the former until 1912 and the latter until 1942.

At the end of the 20th century, Parliament undertook a thorough revision of the Constitution. Approved by popular vote on 18 April 1999, the new version came into effect on 1 January 2000. It is very similar in form and substance to the 1874 text.

The new 1874 provisions

- An **optional referendum** ("*référendum facultatif – fakultative Referendum*") was introduced, requiring any law passed by Parliament to be submitted to a popular vote if at least 30,000 citizens requested it (50,000 from 1977).

The right of the people to propose modifications of the Constitution by referendum has existed since 1881: proposed changes to the Constitution then required 50,000 signatures (100,000 from 1977) for submission to a popular vote (that required a "double majority" to pass – see preceding paragraph).

- The cantons retained only very limited authority in military matters.

- Compulsory (secular) primary education was introduced. Education became the responsibility of the cantons.

- The creation of new convents and monasteries was forbidden. Jesuits were banned from all clerical and teaching activities.

- The **Federal Tribunal**, established in 1848, changed from a rotating location to a permanent headquarters in Lausanne. The Federal Parliament appoints the judges.

- Registration of births, marriages and deaths (including cemeteries) was taken over by the cantonal civil (non-religious) authorities.

In 1848, the Radicals held power in Switzerland almost on their own: they had all the seats in the Federal Council and an overwhelming majority in Parliament. In 1891, they had to give a seat in government to the Catholic-Conservatives (fore-runners of the Christian Democrats). The Radical party kept its majority until 1919, when proportional representation was intro-duced (····⟩ p. 68). They filled the majority of seats on the Federal Council until 1954.

Foreign relations

With its neutrality confirmed, the Confederation avoided entanglement in any European conflicts, despite occasional tensions with some of its neighbours.

Created as a Swiss initiative, the Red Cross began its work with a large-scale programme of assistance to French soldiers fleeing the defeat of France in 1870.

On the international stage, Switzerland became a mediator and a land of refuge.

Neuchâtel, Savoy and Bourbaki

• From 1815 to 1848, **Neuchâtel** was simultaneously a canton and a principality under the rule of the king of Prussia. In 1848, the Republicans came to power in the canton: Prussia refused to recognise the new government but remained passive. In 1856, royalists attempted a coup d'état. The Federal army intervened and captured the leaders of the revolt. Prussia insisted they be freed, but the Federal Council refused. Both countries started preparing for war. Thanks to British and French mediation, conflict was avoided.

The prisoners were freed and the king of Prussia retained only the symbolic title of "Prince of Neuchâtel."

• In 1860, the Confederation lost a dispute with the French Emperor Napoleon III who was about to annex **Savoy**. Federal Councillor Jakob Stämpfli pressed a claim by Switzerland to the northern part of the territory (Evian, Annemasse and Annecy), to which it had acquired in 1815 a right to send troops for self-defence. A minority of the local population signed a petition to join Switzerland but a referendum confirmed unification with France.

In compensation, a free-trade area (exemption from import duties) was set up around Geneva.

• In 1870, the Franco-German war ended in the rout of the troops of Napoleon III. The Federal army was mobilised at the Swiss frontiers. 85,000 defeated French soldiers, serving under **General Bourbaki** entered Switzerland at the town of Les Verrières (NE). After being disarmed, they were interned and taken care of in various places all over Switzerland. This was the first major campaign of the Red Cross.

Initially pro-German, the Swiss population was touched by the fate of the hungry and wretched French soldiers.

The creation of the Red Cross

- In the 1850s, **Henri Dunant** of Geneva was managing a wheat-milling company in French Algeria. As a result of problems with the French colonial authorities, the company went bankrupt and Dunant went to seek support from Napoleon III, who was then at war with the Austrians at Solferino in Italy.

- When he arrived there, Dunant was faced with the bloody spectacle of thousands of wounded soldiers left to their own devices. In 1862, on his return to Geneva, he published *Un souvenir de Solferino* ("A memoir of Solferino"), in which he proposed the creation of medical aid corps to care for the war-wounded and establish international rules of conduct for their protection.

- A committee was formed, of which Dunant and General Dufour were members. It began by choosing a graphic symbol that would be a visual means of protecting medical personnel during combat: a red cross on a white background.

This was the Swiss flag in reverse (⋯⟩ p. 22), although there is no record that this was the idea behind the design.

FOR THE NEW RED CROSS!

- The International Committee of the Red Cross **(ICRC)** was set up in 1863. It organised an international conference in Geneva in August 1864, at which a "Convention for the Amelioration of the Condition of the Wounded in Armies in the Field" was adopted. This was the first step in establishing international humanitarian law.

The creation of the Red Cross was the beginning of Switzerland's commitment to international affairs; today many international organisations have their headquarters in the country – especially in Geneva.

A land of refuge

Switzerland allowed many foreign political dissidents to enter the country. Their governments regularly pressed the Confederation to return them, but without success.

For example: – The French citizen Gambetta, an opponent of Napoleon III: Clarens (VD) has a square and an avenue bearing his name;

– The French painter Courbet, active in the Paris Commune (the aborted revolution of 1871), died at La Tour-de-Peilz (VD) in 1877;

– The Russian revolutionary Lenin lived intermittently in Switzerland (mainly in Zurich and Geneva) between 1900 and 1917.

From the end of the 19th century until today, Switzerland has played the role of mediator in international conflicts. In 1900, for example, the President of the Confederation, Walter Hauser, arbitrated a long-standing territorial dispute between Brazil and France. French Guiana has a common frontier with Brazil. Hauser declared in favour of the latter, and France conceded a large area of territory.

Economy and Society

With the development of industry, infrastructure, services and quality of life, Switzerland became wealthier.

The economy specialised in high value-added sectors. The most complex rail network in the world was built. Tourism became a real industry.

However, part of the population remained impoverished and chose emigration to other continents.

In 1856, the planned route of the railway between Geneva and Bern caused disagreement between the government of Vaud and the city of Lausanne. Vaud wanted a line through Yverdon and Morat, which would have been easier to build but would not have passed through Lausanne. The city insisted on a line further east, from Lausanne to Fribourg. The latter was chosen.

THE TRAIN FOR SWITZERLAND WILL BE DELAYED BY SEVERAL YEARS!

An industrialised country

- Switzerland, like other European countries, underwent an **industrial revolution** in the 19th century. Watch-making (in the Jura arc) and textiles (in the north and east of the country) were predominant. From 1848, the centralisation of the government (····⟩ p. 55) facilitated economic growth.

- With neither raw materials nor access to seaports, the country specialised in high-value business: chemicals, food products, mechanical engineering, banking, insurance.

  For example:

  – *around 1860, Henri Nestlé, a German refugee, invented in Vevey a product combining flour and milk for mothers who could not breast-feed their babies; Nestlé became a multinational company;*

  – *around 1880, Julius Maggi, the son of an Italian immigrant, and Fridolin Schuler, a Swiss, marketed powdered soups (Maggi is today part of Nestlé);*

  – *founded between 1860 and 1870, the Winterthur and Thurgau banks, together with the Basel Trade Bank, were the distant ancestors of UBS, today one of the largest banks in the world.*

Transport

- From 1815, coach roads were built through the Alps. In 1823, the first steamship crossed the Lac Léman.

- The **railway** was late to arrive in Switzerland. The first line (Zurich- Baden) was inaugurated in 1847. From 1854 to 1864, 1300 kilometres of railroad were built with private capital. At the end of the century, the country had the most highly developed rail network in the world.

- The construction of the **Gotthard tunnel** (1872-1882) made it possible to cross the Alps by rail. It was a remarkable technical achievement at the time. The Simplon tunnel was completed in 1906 and the Lötschberg in 1913.

- In 1902, the Confederation purchased most private rail companies and created a national corporation: the Swiss Federal Railways (*CFF* in French, *SBB* in German and *FFS* in Italian).

Fewer and fewer agricultural workers

- Around 1850, approximately two-thirds of the population depended on agricultural employment. However, this proportion was on the decrease and represented only 25% by 1914.

  Today, 3-4% of the population are employed in agriculture.

- Rural communities were frequently very poor. Farming the land was physically demanding, brought little income and competed with cheap grain imports. There was a shift to dairy farming, which was less exhausting and brought a better return.

Emigration

- Many Swiss emigrated during the 19th century, driven by a combination of factors – principally poverty, rapid population growth, shortage of land and economic problems.

  There was also much immigration into Switzerland. Many foreigners, especially Italians, came to work on major public works projects, such as the Gotthard tunnel.

- With the support of the authorities (who were able in this way to rid themselves of impoverished inhabitants they were otherwise obliged to support) groups from the same canton left together. Swiss colonies were set up all over the world, especially in the Americas.

  For example: Vevay (USA 1803), Nova Friburgo (Brazil 1815), New Glarus (USA 1845), Nueva Helvecia (Uruguay 1861).

In the 19th century, technical progress radically changed daily life, at least in the towns. Around 1860, **running water** systems (in which the British were pioneers) were installed in houses; rural communities had to wait for these facilities until 1945. Running water made possible the introduction of **flush toilets** (another British invention). In the 1880s, electricity was installed in homes, and replaced gas for street lighting. The **telephone**, an American invention, arrived in Switzerland at the end of the 1870s. The first telephone line linked the psychiatric hospital and the public health service in Lausanne.

Tourism

- After 1850, tourism developed in Switzerland. The railway network made travel easier and wealthy customers (mainly English) were attracted by the landscapes, winter sports and spas.

  The area around the Lac Léman (Geneva, Lausanne-Ouchy, Vevey-Montreux), the Alps (Zermatt, St. Moritz) and Ticino (Lugano) were the favourite tourist spots.

- Luxury hotels and boarding schools for the children of wealthy foreigners were established. Alpine railways were built – many were, for the period, remarkable feats of engineering (e.g. in 1912, a cog railway was built up to the Jungfraujoch at 3,400m).

  Farmers from mountain areas became guides or opened hotels.

COME ON DAISY, MOVE ALONG THERE!

HE WAS A COWHERD BEFORE HE BECAME A GUIDE!

1838-1914

The labour movement

Economic development led to the growth of a working class; unions were set up for the protection of workers' rights.

The appearance of the "Union Syndicale Suisse/Schweizerischer Gewerkschaftsbund" (Swiss Trade Union Confederation) and later of the Socialist Party, influenced by Marxism, added a new dimension to national politics.

Working conditions and wage levels gradually improved.

In 1832, cottage textile workers at Uster (ZH) set fire to a new factory that was competing with them; they had just gone into debt to buy new weaving equipment.

Exploited workers

- During the second half of the 19th century, Switzerland's industrial development and wealth increased. However, the benefits went mainly to the employers: the labour force had to work under very difficult conditions.

- Before 1850, the working day was 14 or 15 hours and wages were a pittance. Workshop discipline was harsh. Children as young as 7 were employed on arduous tasks. There was little concern for health and safety at the workplace.

- **Socialist** ideas promulgated the protection of labour against the growing power of capital. After 1848 and the aborted revolutions in Europe, political movements for the defence of the working class (proletariat) gained strength, inspired by the ideas of the German thinker **Karl Marx**. He saw class war as a means for emancipating the proletariat.

The first militants

- From 1838, the Geneva Grütli Association (*Société du Grütli*) was formed to fight for improvements in workers' lives.

- In the 1860s and 1870s, many foreigners fled to Switzerland (and especially to Geneva) to escape persecution in their home countries for their trade union activities. They contributed to the growth of the Swiss labour movement.

  - German workers, in exile in Switzerland, pressed for the formation in the Suisse Romande of sections of the International Workingmen's Association (IWA, also known as the First International), which held its inaugural Congress in Geneva in 1866.

  - The Russian anarchist, Mikhail Bakunin, who had found refuge in the Suisse Romande, spread his ideas in some sections of the IWA: e.g. individual freedom and destruction of the State.

IT'S TOUGH...

... BEING THE FIRST TO FIGHT FOR YOUR RIGHTS!

UNITED WE STAND

One trade union and one party

- The Swiss Labour Federation (Fédération Ouvrière Suisse), founded in 1873, became the Swiss Trade Union Confederation (*Union Syndicale Suisse* – USS; *Schweizerischer Gewerkschaftsbund* – SGB) in 1880. The Swiss Labour Conference created the Socialist Party (PS) in 1888. The first Socialist member of Parliament was elected in Zurich in 1890.

  Left-wing activities forced the other political forces to reorganise themselves. The Radical Party (PRD) and the Catholic People's Party (forerunner of the Christian Democrats, PDC) were set up in 1894.

- The **USS/SGB** took off in the 1890s. Half its members were foreigners, especially Germans and Italians. Without any rights, these foreign members radicalised the organisation in favour of class war, and organised many strikes.

  In 1912, a General Strike – the first in Switzerland – paralysed the city of Zurich for several days.

- The **Socialist Party** also moved further to the left. In 1904, it adopted a Marxist programme aiming at proletarian revolution.

Social policy

- The trade unions achieved an improvement in workers' lives. From 1850 to 1914, wages increased four-fold in absolute terms (the relative increase was less because prices were also rising).

- In 1848, Glarus became the first canton to put a social policy into effect: a maximum working day of 13 hours, prohibition of employment of children under 12, and measures to improve health and safety at the workplace.

- In 1877, a Federal Factory Law was adopted by referendum: 11-hour working day, prohibition of child labour under age 14, worker protection and factory inspections.

  The policy was ferociously opposed by the employers. It was the first major political victory for the left.

- In 1912, health insurance was introduced by law, although it was not compulsory. Employers had, however, to insure their workers against accidents.

  The first collective bargaining agreements were reached around 1910.

The increasing number of social protests (for example, the 1868 strike of building workers in Geneva, or that of the masons in Lausanne in 1869) forced employers to create organisations for negotiating with the unions. In 1870, they set up the **Swiss Association of Trade and Industry** (in French, *Union Suisse du commerce et de l'industrie*; in German, *Schweizerischer Handels- und Industrie-Verein*) that was known from 1882 by the acronym Vorort. In 2000, it was renamed *economiesuisse*. In 1882, a group of small companies and artisans broke away and formed the **Swiss Association of Arts and Professions** (in French *Union suisse des arts et métiers usam*; in German, *Schweizerische Gewerbeverband sgv*). Bern very quickly proposed subsidies to these powerful organisations, in exchange for their help in formulating social and economic policies.

The 20th century
(1914 to the present)

World War I

Switzerland was surrounded by warring countries and armed itself to protect its neutrality if the need arose.

There were tensions between the German-speaking Swiss – more favourable to Germany – and the French-speakers – closer to France. The war created economic problems. In 1918 a general strike was called.

At the end of the conflict, advances were made in social policy.

General Wille, commander of the Swiss army from 1914-1918, was not much liked by French-speakers in Switzerland. A supporter of Prussian military methods (his wife Clara was a descendant of the Bismarck family in Germany), he wrote to the Federal Council on 20 July 1915 suggesting that Switzerland should enter the war on the German side. The correspondence was leaked to the press, creating a scandal in the Suisse Romande.

TRENCH WARFARE

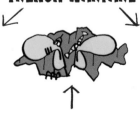

ENTRENCHED PEACE

Neutrality in question

- In the summer of 1914, the assassination at **Sarajevo** of the heir to the Austro-Hungarian throne ignited a generalised European conflict. An alliance of the "Central Powers" (Germany, Austria-Hungary and Turkey) were opposed by an alliance comprising Russia, France, Great Britain and Italy (the "Allies").

- For the first time since 1815, Switzerland was surrounded by countries at war. As provided by the Constitution in cases of conflict, on 8 April 1914 the Federal Parliament appointed a General to command the army, in the person of Colonel **Ulrich Wille**.

- Switzerland confirmed its **neutrality** and General Wille implemented a defensive strategy for the protection of the country. The forces (varying at times between 30,000 and 100,000) were concentrated in the areas closest to the fighting: the Franco-German front at Ajoie (near Porrentruy in today's Jura canton); and the Austro-Italian front in the lower Engadine valley (Graubünden).

- The country was well prepared for defence, but not for the economic effects of war. The absence of raw materials slowed industrial activity and the population suffered as a result.

  Business recovered subsequently and Swiss exports to the opposing sides were very profitable.

- French-speaking Swiss were shocked by the pro-German tendencies of the commander of the Swiss army and a gulf grew between the two main linguistic groups of the country (the words "fossé" in French and "Graben" in German were already used at this time to describe this phenomenon – later described as the *Röstigraben* (····> pp. 15 and 81).

- A number of scandals excited public opinion in the Suisse Romande.
  For example:
  - *at the end of 1915, two Swiss officers received only light sentences for having communicated strategic information on the Allies to the Germans and Austrians;*
  - *in June 1917, Federal Councillor Arthur Hoffmann was persuaded by a socialist member of the Swiss Parliament (Robert Grimm) to mediate in separate peace discussions between Russia and Germany; this would have allowed Germany to divert all its forces against France. Hoffmann was forced to resign.*

The General Strike of 1918

- The war created economic problems, especially for the urban working class. Mobilised soldiers often lost their jobs and received no compensation. Prices escalated, **unemployment** rose and wages dropped.

- The Socialist Party and the USS/SGB responded vigorously to this **crisis**. From 1916, the number of demonstrations and strikes increased. In February 1918, militants set up an action committee called the "Olten Committee."

In 1915, Lenin attended an international socialist conference at Zimmerwald (BE). The revolutionary positions put forward there influenced leftist circles in Switzerland.

- With the collapse of Germany in November 1918, the Swiss army – fearing a revolutionary **insurrection** – occupied Zurich. This led to a call for a General Strike. On 11 November (Armistice Day), 250,000 people stopped work. The Federal Council issued an ultimatum and after three days the strikers, under threat from the army, went back to work.

The strike was followed mainly in German-speaking towns. In the Suisse Romande, the victory of France captured popular enthusiasm.

The consequences of the strike

- The strike was put down without much violence, but the Federal Council was concerned about the possibility of a revolution on the Russian model (the Bolsheviks had seized power in 1917). The army was on constant alert. Tensions remained until 1919, when there were widely supported local strikes in Zurich and Basel.

- The workers obtained a partial success: a working week of **48 hours** and wage increases. Other social measures followed.

In 1925, a provision for old-age pensions was inserted in the Constitution. A full system of retirement pensions (AVS in French – AHV in German) had to wait until 1948.

After the war, the Austrian province of Vorarlberg requested admission as the 23rd Swiss canton. This was confirmed by a provincial referendum in which 47,000 voted for and 11,000 against. However, the Federal Council and Parliament rejected the request: French-speaking cantons and Protestants were concerned that it would strengthen the influence of the German-speakers and Catholics. The Principality of Liechtenstein, situated between Switzerland and Vorarlberg, concluded a Customs Union with Switzerland in 1919 and adopted the Swiss currency and postal system.

1918-1939

The inter-war period

After the war, two major economic crises slowed economic development in Switzerland.

A new electoral system changed the political balance in favour of the left. Employers and unions concluded a "labour peace."

Faced with the growth of different forms of fascism, Switzerland prepared for another war.

A new political balance of forces

- After two refusals (in 1900 and 1910) Swiss voters accepted – just before the strikes of 1918 – the introduction of **proportional representation** (in place of majority voting) for elections to the National Council. This favoured the smaller parties.

  In contrast to the German-speaking cantons, the Suisse Romande was very much in favour of this type of voting. In the period 1891-1921, sixteen cantons adopted the proportional method for elections to the cantonal Parliament ("Grand Conseil"). Majority voting was kept for elections to the Council of States, in which there is still a substantial rightist majority today.

- In 1919, in the first proportional elections, the Radicals lost the absolute majority they had held since 1848. The Conservative-Catholics (the future Christian Democrats PDC) and the Socialists each won about a quarter of the seats. The Peasants, Artisans and Self-employed Party (PAI – future Swiss People's Party UDC/SVP) had a few less. Radicals, Conservatives and the PAI formed an antisocialist "bourgeois bloc."

- After the introduction of proportional voting, a second representative of the Conservative-Catholics joined the Federal Council in 1920. Radicals held only five seats – and then four, when an Agrarian (PAI) representative was elected in 1929; the right opposed a seat in government for the Socialists.

The League of Nations

- After the First World War, the **Treaty of Versailles** redrew the map of Europe (1919). It reconfirmed Swiss neutrality.

- The victorious allies created the League of Nations (LN – the predecessor of the UN), with headquarters in Geneva. They invited Switzerland to join and there was a lively debate about whether membership was compatible with Swiss neutrality. In 1920, the people and cantons voted with a narrow majority in favour of joining.

  Switzerland opted for "differential neutrality" – no armed sanctions against a country, only economic measures.

Crises and labour peace

- Switzerland was hit heavily by two serious **economic crises** during the periods 1920-1925 and 1930-1936.

  In 1936 there were 124,000 unemployed, 7% of the active population.

- Textiles, watch-making and banking suffered. The Federal Council devalued the Franc to promote exports and reduce unemployment. A **federal income tax** ("Impôt Fédéral Direct") was introduced alongside cantonal income tax.

  Other economic sectors, such as mechanical engineering, suffered less – mainly thanks to investment in the electrification of the railway network in the 1920s. The development of hydro-power (from dams in the Alps) made Switzerland energy-independent.

- Swiss neutrality provided financial stability between 1914 and 1918. From the 1920s, the Swiss financial services business grew substantially, becoming one of largest in the world – especially as a refuge for foreign capital. **Banking secrecy**, frequently linked to tax evasion, was widely practiced by Swiss banks during several decades before being enshrined in the banking law of 1934.

- In 1937, unions and employers signed a **"labour peace agreement"** that encouraged conciliation and arbitration of labour disputes.

Fascism and neutrality

- From 1922 in Italy (**Benito Mussolini**) and 1933 in Germany (**Adolf Hitler**), fascists came to power (authoritarian and strongly nationalist government). In Switzerland, extreme rightist "fronts" came on the political scene but had little success in elections.

  Fascism was feared less than communism (Switzerland had not yet recognised the Soviet Union). In 1937, the University of Lausanne granted an honorary doctorate to Mussolini.

- After 1935, international relations were marked by much tension. Europe (and Switzerland) was preparing for war. The League of Nations had become toothless. In 1938, the Confederation **reverted** to a policy of "absolute" (as opposed to "differential") neutrality.

  After the Italian invasion of Abyssinia (Ethiopia), Switzerland refused to apply the economic sanctions imposed by the League against Mussolini.

On the evening of 9 November 1932, a leftist demonstration took place in a big square in Geneva *(Plainpalais)*, protesting against a meeting of the *Union Nationale,* a fascist and anti-Semitic movement led by the writer Géo Oltramare. At the request of the Geneva government, a battalion of young recruits was sent from Lausanne to restore order. They fired on the crowd: 13 were killed and more than 60 wounded. In the 1933 elections, the left gained a majority in the Geneva government.

World War II

Surrounded by countries at war, Switzerland organised its defence and daily life.

Mobilised, the army guarded the frontiers. In case of attack, it was to withdraw to a "national redoubt" in the heart of the Alps. The Wahlen plan provided food for all.

Switzerland suffered almost no material or economic consequences from the war.

On 25 July 1940, General Guisan brought all senior Swiss officers together on the Rütli meadow (····> p. 21). He gave a speech of which there is no record. What mattered first and foremost was the symbolism of the place. He called on the troops to "stand fast" and offered a first outline of the strategy of the "national redoubt."

Mobilisation

- On 1 September 1939, Nazi Germany invaded Poland and ignited the Second World War, involving the Axis Powers (Germany, Italy, Japan) and the Allies (France, Great Britain, USA, USSR).

  Switzerland was surrounded: Germany to the north and east (Hitler annexed Austria in 1938); Italy in the south (a combatant from 1940, then occupied by Germany from 1943); France in the west (a combatant in 1939, then occupied by Germany from 1940 to 1944).

- On 30 August 1939, with war imminent, the Swiss Parliament delegated full powers to the Federal Council and – as foreseen in time of war – appointed a General: Colonel **Henri Guisan** from Vaud. On 2 September, the army was fully mobilised. In three days, 430,000 men reported for duty. A mobilisation order went out again on 11 May 1940, after the western offensive by the Germans.

  In a state of panic after the German offensive in France, part of the population of Basel and areas close to the northern border fled in disorder to central Switzerland and the Suisse Romande.

- The two **full mobilisation** orders lasted only a few weeks. For the rest of the time, 150,000 soldiers remained under arms. 80,000 additional men were mobilised during the allied campaigns in Western Europe in the summer of 1944, to prevent transit by belligerents through Swiss territory.

- The Swiss army was only partially prepared for war. New arms and training methods were introduced during the conflict. Overall, discipline and morale were good. However, seventeen soldiers were condemned to death and executed for treason.

  A popular personality, General Guisan embodied the idea of a neutral but armed nation. He had remarkable leadership abilities.

- Swiss airspace was frequently violated. Swiss air defences shot down 23 planes from both camps. In 1944, the Americans bombed Schaffhausen by mistake, causing 40 deaths. Basel, Geneva and the railway station of Renens (VD) were also hit by bombs dropped in error.

The "national redoubt"

- From 1940, the Axis powers surrounded Switzerland, which feared a German invasion.

- According to the "national redoubt" strategy, in case of attack light mobile units would oppose the invaders on the Plateau, while the main force would withdraw to the Alps, protected by three key strongpoints: St. Maurice (VS), Sargans (SG) and the Gotthard. Bridges and tunnels would be destroyed. However, this plan came at a heavy price: withdrawing forces from the plateau meant abandoning three-quarters of the civilian population, the large towns and the main industrial plants. If attacked, the country would still have had a government, but it would have operated from its retreat in the mountains.

A major network of fortifications was built in the Alps to implement the "national redoubt" strategy.

- The Germans prepared plans for the invasion of Switzerland, but never seriously envisaged implementing them: they saw advantages in preserving the industrial capacity and financial services of Switzerland, of which they were major clients (···> p. 73), and in keeping open the transport routes through the Alps.

The war promoted social progress. From end-1939, the Federal Council adopted measures to compensate the effects of the conflict. Mobilised soldiers received an indemnity for loss of income and were protected against loss of their civilian jobs. Rents were frozen and leases could not be cancelled without valid reason. A price control system was introduced and improvements were made in unemployment insurance and family allowances.

The Wahlen plan

- From September 1939, consumer goods were subject to rationing. The Wahlen plan (named after a senior civil servant and subsequent Federal Councillor, who prepared it on his own initiative as early as 1935) provided for the extension of agricultural land and improvements in crop yields.

- The plan was promoted by extensive publicity campaigns under the label "battle of the fields." The aim of Swiss self-sufficiency in basic foodstuffs was never achieved, but the people did not suffer too much from rationing.

The area of cultivated land doubled: crops were planted on pastureland, public parks and sportsgrounds.

POTATOES ON MONDAY... POTATOES ON TUESDAY... POTATOES ON WEDNESDAY TOO

... YOU HAVE JUST HEARD A MESSAGE FROM MR. WAHLEN.

Relations with Germany

Despite its neutrality, Switzerland was subject to fascist pressure – internal as well as external.

The Nazi victories led to disagreement on the political response to the new situation. The continued functioning of the Swiss economy was dependent on exports to Germany.

The continuation of trade with the Nazis was a source of friction with the Allies.

Fascist pressure

- In 1940, after the German victory in France, some people in Switzerland thought that the country should adapt itself to what was called "the **new order**" – the victory of fascism in Europe.

- Just after the signing of the armistice between France and Germany in June, **Marcel Pilet-Golaz** of Vaud, President of the Confederation and Federal Councillor in charge of foreign affairs, gave a speech in which he vaguely suggested the need for an "internal rebirth." Other members of the government were not unfavourably disposed towards fascism.

- Extreme right-wing "fronts" (---> p. 69) reappeared and demanded a transformation of Swiss institutions to reflect the new situation in Europe. Leading figures in economic life were also receptive to these ideas.

- The press – despite censure intended to mollify the Nazis – and some political parties were critical of this tolerance of fascism. Finally, the Federal Council prohibited all extremist parties: fascists and communists.

- After 1940, internal political tensions diminished, even though the style of government remained authoritarian. The war also "sanctified" a new form of national unity with the accession in 1943 of the first socialist to the Federal Council, Ernst Nobs of Zurich.

  Ernst Nobs had been imprisoned for his part in organising the 1918 strikes.

Volunteers on the front

From 1941, Swiss senior officers and diplomats who supported Hitler organised four "medical missions" for the treatment of (German) soldiers on the Russian front. On return, they were forbidden to tell of the atrocities they had witnessed.

Despite the opposition of General Guisan, the Federal Council and the Red Cross gave their approval for these medical missions, on condition that they were undertaken as a purely private initiative.

A good customer

- Switzerland continued to export a large part of its production to Germany. The Confederation exported tools, machines and arms (60% of Swiss arms production in the period 1941-1942 went to Germany) in exchange for raw materials (iron and coal).

- The **Nazis** kept Switzerland under pressure, threatening repeatedly to interrupt trade. The delivery of raw materials was not enough to cover the costs of the goods delivered by Switzerland and the country was forced to accept higher and higher levels of German debt.

  Some limited trading links were kept with Great Britain.

- The Swiss **financial markets** continued to thrive. The Germans traded gold – frequently plundered from occupied territories – for Swiss Francs, which allowed them to purchase raw materials in other countries.

  The Allies also used the Swiss financial marketplace.

- The **Allies** accused Switzerland of contributing to the German war effort. From 1943, they put increasing pressure on the Confederation to reduce trade with its neighbour. Switzerland complied, but only in stages. On 8 March 1945, two months before the end of the war, the Allies and Switzerland signed an agreement ending trade with Germany.

On 9 April 1941, the Federal Council decreed the establishment of a Swiss navy. Cut off by hostilities from its traditional supply routes (for example, from Mediterranean ports), the Confederation was forced to purchase ocean-going vessels to fly the Swiss flag and thus operate in relative safety. Today, the Swiss navy has some 25 vessels, based in different European ports (including an oil tanker) and nearly 300 barges for navigation on the Rhine from the port of Basel.

1939-1945
Rewriting history

Since the 1990s, Switzerland has been re-assessing its attitude towards Nazi Germany.

Was it morally acceptable for the Swiss to trade with the Nazis and refuse entry to Jews at the frontiers? The banks – the target of very strong criticism – were forced to identify all amounts held in "dormant" (unclaimed) accounts opened by victims of the Nazi regime and reimburse the survivors or their heirs.

In January 1997, Christoph Meili, a night-watchman at UBS in Zurich, discovered that documents about dormant (unclaimed) accounts were being destroyed. The press caught wind of the affair and Meili was prosecuted for infringing the bank secrecy law. He finally sought political asylum in the USA, where he settled with his family before returning to Switzerland in 2009.

THIS IS THE KIND OF SHADY PAGE WE WOULD RATHER FORGET !

Switzerland accused

- From 1935, Nazi Germany organised the segregation and systematic annihilation of Jews. Some six million died in concentration and extermination camps.

- After the war, Swiss historians projected the image of Switzerland as a small neutral country that had maintained armed resistance, alone in the centre of the storm. Little by little, however, a debate began on the morality of the Swiss attitude to the Nazi regime, calling for reassessment of this narrative.

- From 1995, the USA and the **World Jewish Congress** expressed harsh criticism of Switzerland with the following arguments:
  - Switzerland had received gold plundered by the Nazis;
  - Swiss banks had kept in their vaults large sums of money deposited by Jews who had perished in the Holocaust ("dormant accounts");
  - the authorities had turned Jews away at the frontiers, thereby condemning them to certain death;
  - because of its economic ties to Germany, Switzerland had contributed to the Nazi war effort and prolonged the war (⤑ p. 73).

- Under pressure, the Federal Council set up on 13 December 1996 an independent committee of experts on Switzerland's role in the Second World War, known as the **Bergier Committee**, from the name of its Chairman, the historian Jean-François Bergier. Its mandate was to shed light on relations between Switzerland and Germany in the period 1933-1945. The "Bergier report" was published at the end of 2001.

- At the end of 1998, under threat of boycott because of the scandal of the dormant accounts, Swiss banks concluded a global settlement under which they returned 1.25 billion dollars to the rightful claimants.

In 1946, the USA forced Switzerland to pay 58 million dollars to a Tripartite Gold Commission set up by the Allies (in part compensation for the looted gold it had accepted) and to hand over a portion of German assets held in Switzerland.

Refugees

- An island of freedom in occupied Europe, Switzerland attracted refugees, including Jews fleeing Nazi persecution. However, the asylum policy of the Confederation was very restrictive. From 1933, asylum seekers had to provide evidence of not only racial but also political persecution.

  In 1938, Switzerland proposed to Nazi Germany to stamp the passports of German Jews with the letter "J."

- The extermination of Jews by the Nazis was well known in Switzerland. Yet the authorities made it difficult for them to obtain refugee status. **"The boat is full,"** was the expression used in 1942 by Federal Councillor Eduard von Steiger. Parliament, cantons and armed forces supported government policy. There was not much disagreement by the population. The frontiers were opened only from July 1944.

- According to the "Bergier Report," Switzerland accepted 60,000 civilian refugees between 1939 and 1945, of which scarcely half were Jews. Some historians dispute this figure.

  Some 100,000 combatants (mainly French and Polish) were admitted to Switzerland as refugees.

- The number of refugees turned back at the frontier is more difficult to assess: the Bergier Committee reported a total of 20,000 – mainly Jews. This figure is also disputed.

Some Swiss stood out by rescuing Jews condemned to certain death. The most famous was Paul Grüninger, commander of the police force of St. Gallen, who defied the law in permitting refugees to enter Switzerland in 1938-1939. Prosecuted and convicted, he was posthumously rehabilitated only in 1995. Carl Lutz is less well-known: thanks to his diligence as Swiss Consul in Budapest, he saved tens of thousands of lives. He was rehabilitated during his lifetime, in 1958.

The debate goes on...

- While not claiming to provide full answers to all questions, the Bergier Report drew up a relatively critical assessment of Swiss behaviour during the war.

  Some revelations in the Bergier Report:

  - *thanks to the commercial acumen of the Swiss railways and the support of the Railworkers Union, rail transit across the Alps between Germany and Italy contributed to the Nazi war effort;*
  - *at least 11,000 foreign deportees – civil and military prisoners of war – were forced to work in German branches of Swiss companies (Maggi, Brown Boveri, Nestlé) and were often exploited and given inadequate food and shelter.*

- Some people, especially among the war generation, consider that Switzerland owes no one an explanation of its history and that the past can only be judged by reference to the situation prevailing at the time.

1945-1975

Thirty golden years – the economic miracle

The immediate post-war period was marked by thirty years of economic prosperity in Switzerland.

Industry was working at full capacity and called on a significant pool of foreign labour. These workers, although essential for the economy, were sometimes discriminated against by the local population.

Despite being firmly in the Western camp, Switzerland traded with the communist bloc while at the same time arming itself against a possible Soviet invasion.

In the 1990s, immigrants from Italy were replaced by workers from the Balkans. The wars in Yugoslavia led to the arrival of many Bosnian, Croat, Kosovan, Serb and other refugees. Refugee policy is now at the centre of the debate on immigration. In 2020, 25% of the inhabitants of Switzerland – and 31% of the working population – were foreigners. A third of the population has an immigrant background.

Economic prosperity

Switzerland was one of the only European countries to come out of the war with its industry intact. In contrast to 1918, the much-feared crisis did not occur. On the contrary, the country enjoyed thirty years of prosperity: known as the economic miracle.

During the 1960s, the Swiss economy operated at full capacity; a phenomenon known as "overheating." Consumers benefited and wealth increased but the Federal Council had to adopt urgent measures to fight inflation (price rises).

Immigration

- In the space of a century, the population of Switzerland more than doubled, from 3.3 million in 1900 to 7.2 million in 2000. Higher life expectancy partially balanced a fall in the birth rate: couples had fewer children but lived longer.

- The large numbers of immigrants also filled the gap created by the falling Swiss birth rate. Foreign workers – mainly Italian, but also Spanish and Portuguese, came to seek work in Switzerland. The country welcomed them with open arms, since the economy was facing a labour shortage.

- In the 1960s, the overheating of the economy, problems of integration and **xenophobia** in certain circles led the authorities to place limits on immigration.

In 1970, the "Schwarzenbach initiative," named after a leader of the extreme right, which aimed to counteract what it called "an excess of foreigners" (Überfremdung in German) was rejected by the narrow margin of 54%. In 1968 and 1974, two similar initiatives were rejected by larger margins.

Transport and energy

- The **railways** remained well-networked and modern, even if some small secondary lines were threatened or abandoned. Switzerland began to build freeways as of 1959, beginning with the Geneva-Lausanne link. Road tunnels were dug – including the Great St. Bernard, opened in 1964, the first to go through the Alps.

Switzerland continued to burrow beneath the Alps, and the work has gone on: the Gotthard road tunnel (1980), and the Lötschberg (2007) and Gotthard (2016) rail tunnels were opened.

- Switzerland – the "water-tower of Europe" – makes good use of its hydro-power resources for generating electricity. **Dams** have been built at the foot of valleys – especially in the canton of Valais – creating artificial lakes.

The Grand-Dixence dam – built from 1953-1961 – is the highest dam of its kind in the world: 285m.

Switzerland and the Cold War

- After 1945, the world split into **two opposing blocs**: West v. East (the USA and its allies, on the one hand, and the USSR and its communist satellites on the other). This contest without armed conflict is called the "Cold War." Officially neutral, although fully within the Western camp, Switzerland attempted to pursue its economic interests while maintaining good relations with both sides.

In 1917 the Confederation refused to grant official recognition to the USSR but did so in 1946.

- The Swiss population was quite strongly anti-communist. Public opinion was negatively influenced by two unsuccessful uprisings against communist power: in Hungary (1956) and Czechoslovakia (1968). Switzerland opened its borders to 12,000 refugees from these clashes.

- Fear of a communist invasion of Western Europe also influenced Swiss military strategy: national defence (network of fortifications, modernisation of armaments) was reinforced.

Freeway construction also served military needs. Some sections were designed to be used for take-off and landing by fighter planes.

After 1945, the Federal Council favoured acquisition by Switzerland of an atomic option as part of its defence strategy. In the mid-1950s, the Confederation purchased, in absolute secrecy, 10 tons of uranium from Great Britain; half was made available to the army. In 1959, Switzerland asked France – still in secret – to help it "with atomic arms." However, from the mid 1960s, the Federal Council finally opted to concentrate on conventional armaments. Nuclear power-stations were nevertheless developed for electricity generation.

SYMBOL OF POST-WAR AFFLUENCE

SYMBOL OF THE COLD WAR

1945 to the present

Political developments

After the war Switzerland enjoyed a long period of stability.

The granting of the vote to women in 1971 and the creation of a new canton (the 23rd) in the Jura in 1979 stimulated public interest in politics.

From 1959, the country was governed by a coalition comprising the main parties of left and right, acting on the principle of compromise.

Until 1961, the Swiss national anthem was entitled "Rufst du mein Vaterland" ("When You call, my Country"), a text written in 1911 by Johann Wyss of Bern, and sung to the tune of "God Save the Queen." In 1981, the Federal Council changed the anthem to "Cantique suisse" ("Swiss hymn") composed in 1841 by Alberyk Zwyssig of Uri, with a text by Leonhard Widmer of Zurich.

IT'S ONLY SINCE 1971 THAT MEN VOTE LIKE THEIR WIVES!

The reign of compromise

- From 1954 to 1958 the Socialists were no longer represented on the Federal Council: Max Weber of Zurich resigned in 1953 after his financial programme was rejected by voters. Now in opposition, they claimed two seats. In 1958, Parliament elected two representatives each from the Conservative-Christian-Social People's Party (future Christian Democratic People's Party - CVP in German and PDC in French), the Radicals (Free Democratic Party - FDP/PLR) and the Socialists (Social Democratic Party - SP/PS), together with one "Agrarian" representative (future Swiss People's Party - SVP/UDC). This so-called **"magic formula"** for government – characterised by the search for compromise and the minimisation of political confrontation, but also by a more time-consuming decision-making process – survived until 2003.

In 1970, the Conservative-Christian-Social People's Party (formerly the Catholic-Conservative Party) changed its name to Christian Democratic People's Party (CVP/PDC). In 1971, the "Agrarian" Party of Farmers, Traders and Independents (BGB/PAI) became the Swiss People's Party (SVP/UDC).

- During the 1990s, left-right divergences led to a hardening of political positions. The **SVP/UDC** adopted a more nationalistic stance and took a hard line on issues such as law and order. Within a few years it had doubled its number of votes – mainly at the expense of the Radicals and Christian Democrats. In 2003, it obtained a second seat on the Federal Council, ousting one of the Christian Democrat representatives.

Smaller parties struggled to survive: extreme right, Communists, Independents, Ecologists. The latter, formed in the 1970s under the banner of the "Green Party," are today relatively strong.

Votes for women

Switzerland was late to implement some social measures, such as the vote for women. In 1959, a first attempt to impose it at Federal level failed. In the same year, however, Vaud and Neuchâtel introduced it at their cantonal level. Geneva followed in 1960. Gradually, the other cantons followed suit. It was implemented for Federal voting in 1971.

In Appenzell, it was only in 1989-90 that women obtained the vote at cantonal level: in the half-canton Ausserrhoden, the Landsgemeinde (Popular Assembly) approved it in 1989; in Innerrhoden it was forced on the half-canton by a decision of the Federal Supreme Court in 1990.

A new canton – Jura

- As of 1815, the former bishopric of Basel (present districts of Jura, Bernese Jura and the Laufen valley) became part of the canton of Bern. From 1945, there was growing popular agitation for secession from Bern and the creation of a 23rd Swiss canton. The arguments became heated and the separatists took action that was not far from terrorism.

JU

- After a first refusal in 1959, the population of the region accepted in 1970 the principle of autonomy. In 1974, they voted narrowly for secession. However, Bern insisted on voting at district and communal level, to ascertain which of these were genuinely in favour.

- The Catholic north decided for a new canton, while the Protestant south opted to remain with Bern. In 1978, a vote at Federal level formalised the creation of the canton of Jura, with effect from 1 January 1979.

  The Laufen valley, German-speaking and Catholic, remained with Bern for a time but chose in 1994 to become part of the half-canton of Basel Country.

- In 2021, voters in the town of Moutier decided to secede from Bern and join the canton of Jura. The change will come into effect at the earliest in 2026.

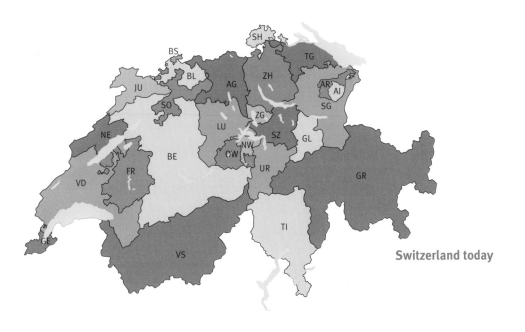

Switzerland today

Switzerland and the world

The fall of communism forced a change in the foreign policy of the Confederation.

Already very active on the international scene through its services as a mediator and "honest broker," Switzerland joined the United Nations in 2002. However, the country did not join the European Union.

Since the 1990s, Switzerland has had to find responses to the challenges of globalisation.

The national airline company, *Swissair* (founded in 1931), had long served as a showcase for Swiss perfectionism. On 2 October 2001 the unthinkable happened: its planes were grounded. A victim of weak economic conditions but also of the company's catastrophic acquisition strategy that cost billions of Francs, *Swissair* was suddenly bankrupt. A new company, *Swiss*, was set up.

International organisations

- In 1945, the victorious Allies set up the United Nations **(UN)**, successor to the League of Nations, with a mandate to maintain world peace and security. Switzerland did not join but offered Geneva as the European headquarters of the UN.

  Geneva became the headquarters of dozens of international organisations active in many different fields (political, economic, technical, humanitarian).

- The Federal Council revised its position on UN membership but, in 1986, encountered a resounding refusal from the electorate. A new vote took place in 2002, resulting in a narrow victory (54% of the popular vote and 12 cantons in favour, 11 against) and Switzerland joined the UN.

  From 1945, Switzerland joined many international organisations, including several UN specialised agencies.

- On occasion, the Confederation was able either to act as a mediator in international conflicts or to represent the interests of States that have suspended diplomatic relations (USA-Cuba, USA-Iran): Switzerland acted as an **"honest broker."**

A new face

After 1989, with the fall of communism, Switzerland had to adapt to the new international order. International activity increased but was focussed more on mandates from the UN.

Since 1999, a contingent from the Swiss armed forces (known as Swisscoy) has participated in international peace-keeping operations in Kosovo (in former Yugoslavia). Following a 2001 referendum on the issue, Swiss soldiers now carry arms for self-defence in such operations.

Globalisation and self-doubt

From the 1990s, Switzerland suffered from the ups and downs of globalisation. Job losses, unemployment (especially in the French-speaking cantons), bankruptcies, mergers and outsourcing created a feeling of insecurity. The Swiss model of perfection, believed by many to be steady as a rock, was put to the test.

A GROUNDED AIRLINE IS EASIER TO BURY !

Switzerland in Europe

- From the end of the Second World War, the countries of Western Europe sought ways of joining forces. This process of "European integration" led to the creation of the European Economic Community (EEC) in 1957, which became the **European Union** (EU) in 1992.

- Switzerland was unwilling to jeopardise its independence and **neutrality** by joining supranational organisations and did not participate in setting up the EEC. In 1959, Switzerland was one of the founders of the European Free Trade Association (EFTA), which imposed less constraints on its members.

  In 1947, Switzerland joined the Organisation for Economic Cooperation and Development (OECD – at that time called the OEEC) and, in 1963, the Council of Europe, which had been set up in 1949.

- In 1992, Switzerland changed direction: the Federal Council put in an application to join the EU. On 6 December, however, membership in a European Economic Area (EEA, grouping EEC and EFTA and – from a Swiss viewpoint – offering a kind of intermediate solution) was rejected by voters (50.3%) and by the cantons (16 to 7). The issue led to a lively debate and revived sentiments related to the **"Röstigraben"** (····⟩ pp. 15 and 66) separating, on the one hand, French-speakers (in general pro-European) and, on the other, German-speakers (mostly opposed).

  There was also a divergence of opinion between urban and rural areas.

- Isolated, Switzerland was forced to negotiate **bilateral agreements** with the EU (free movement of persons, liberalisation of heavy road traffic, mutual recognition of diplomas, etc.). This was the only way of obtaining some of the advantages of membership without actually joining the EU. The agreements came into force in 2002.

  The 1992 application for membership of the EU is now "on ice."

If the Internet was born in the USA in the 1960s, the "World Wide Web - WWW" was actually invented in 1990 at the European Centre (now Organisation) for Nuclear Research (CERN), headquartered near Geneva. Two researchers, Tim Berners-Lee and Robert Cailliau, set up the system known as "hypertext" – a documentary search system ("navigation") that established links to specific documents on different computers. The prefix "www" in Internet addresses is still used for navigation on the Web.

Annexes

Timeline

Switzerland

800 B.C.
Celtic peoples occupied
parts of Switzerland
(······> p. 10)

Approx. 100,000 B.C.
Oldest trace of human
presence in Switzerland
(······> p. 8)

4300 B.C.
Settlements of lake
dwellers on the banks
of some lakes
(······> p. 9)

−3 000 000   −800 000   −200 000   −50 000   −12 000   −3200   −800   −400   −1

Prehistoric   Antiqui

World

2,500,000 B.C.
Homo sapiens
appear in Africa

6000 B.C.
First towns in
Mesopotamia

450 000 B.C.
Domestic use of fire

2600 B.C.
The pyramids were
built in Egypt

753 B.C.
Rome was founded

3000 B.C.
The first writing developed
in Sumer (today's Iraq)

1ST FIRE OF
THE 1ST OF
AUGUST ↘

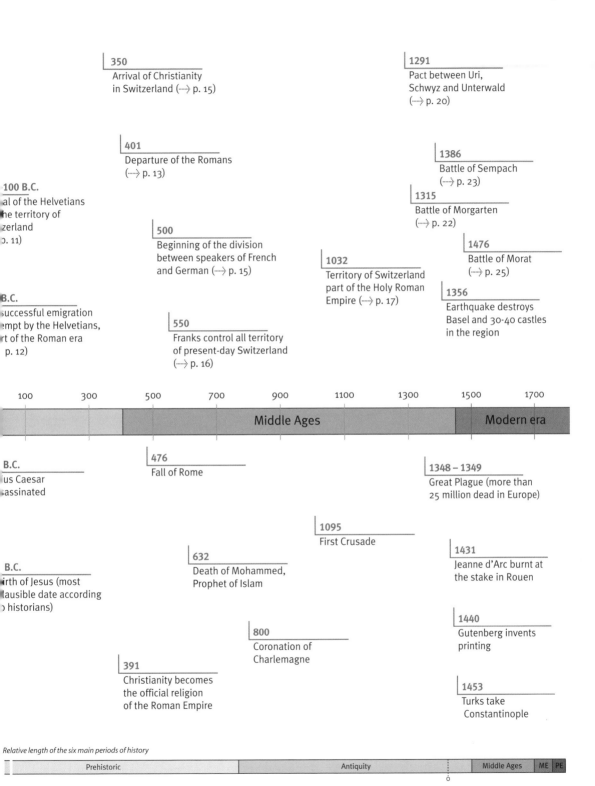

350
Arrival of Christianity
in Switzerland (⤍ p. 15)

1291
Pact between Uri,
Schwyz and Unterwald
(⤍ p. 20)

401
Departure of the Romans
(⤍ p. 13)

1386
Battle of Sempach
(⤍ p. 23)

100 B.C.
al of the Helvetians
he territory of
zerland
0. 11)

1315
Battle of Morgarten
(⤍ p. 22)

500
Beginning of the division
between speakers of French
and German (⤍ p. 15)

1032
Territory of Switzerland
part of the Holy Roman
Empire (⤍ p. 17)

1476
Battle of Morat
(⤍ p. 25)

B.C.
successful emigration
empt by the Helvetians,
rt of the Roman era
p. 12)

1356
Earthquake destroys
Basel and 30-40 castles
in the region

550
Franks control all territory
of present-day Switzerland
(⤍ p. 16)

100	300	500	700	900	1100	1300	1500	1700

Middle Ages | Modern era

476
Fall of Rome

B.C.
us Caesar
assinated

1348 – 1349
Great Plague (more than
25 million dead in Europe)

1095
First Crusade

632
Death of Mohammed,
Prophet of Islam

1431
Jeanne d'Arc burnt at
the stake in Rouen

B.C.
irth of Jesus (most
ausible date according
o historians)

800
Coronation of
Charlemagne

1440
Gutenberg invents
printing

391
Christianity becomes
the official religion
of the Roman Empire

1453
Turks take
Constantinople

Relative length of the six main periods of history

Prehistoric	Antiquity	Middle Ages	ME	PE

Timeline

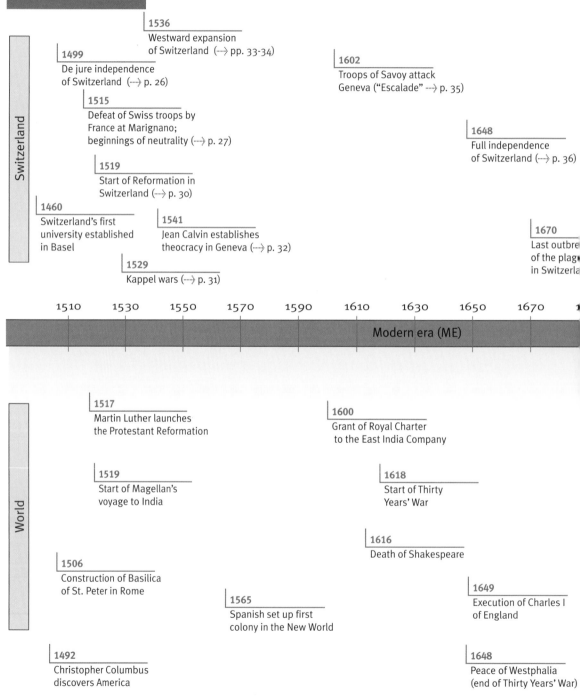

Switzerland

1536
Westward expansion
of Switzerland (----> pp. 33-34)

1499
De jure independence
of Switzerland (----> p. 26)

1515
Defeat of Swiss troops by
France at Marignano;
beginnings of neutrality (----> p. 27)

1519
Start of Reformation in
Switzerland (----> p. 30)

1460
Switzerland's first
university established
in Basel

1541
Jean Calvin establishes
theocracy in Geneva (----> p. 32)

1529
Kappel wars (----> p. 31)

1602
Troops of Savoy attack
Geneva ("Escalade" ----> p. 35)

1648
Full independence
of Switzerland (----> p. 36)

1670
Last outbre
of the plagu
in Switzerla

1510   1530   1550   1570   1590   1610   1630   1650   1670

Modern era (ME)

World

1517
Martin Luther launches
the Protestant Reformation

1519
Start of Magellan's
voyage to India

1506
Construction of Basilica
of St. Peter in Rome

1492
Christopher Columbus
discovers America

1565
Spanish set up first
colony in the New World

1600
Grant of Royal Charter
to the East India Company

1618
Start of Thirty
Years' War

1616
Death of Shakespeare

1649
Execution of Charles I
of England

1648
Peace of Westphalia
(end of Thirty Years' War)

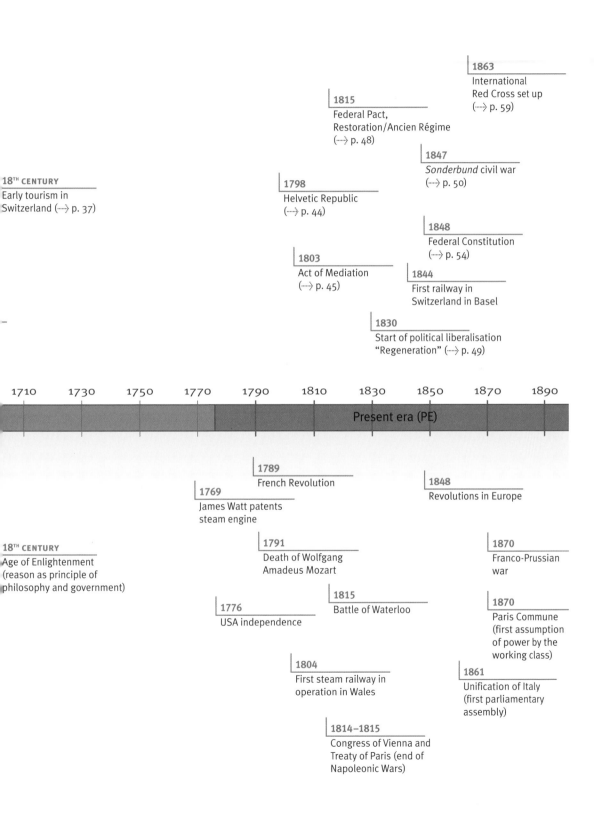

1863
International
Red Cross set up
(---> p. 59)

1815
Federal Pact,
Restoration/Ancien Régime
(---> p. 48)

1847
Sonderbund civil war
(---> p. 50)

18ᵀᴴ CENTURY
Early tourism in
Switzerland (---> p. 37)

1798
Helvetic Republic
(---> p. 44)

1848
Federal Constitution
(---> p. 54)

1803
Act of Mediation
(---> p. 45)

1844
First railway in
Switzerland in Basel

1830
Start of political liberalisation
"Regeneration" (---> p. 49)

1710   1730   1750   1770   1790   1810   1830   1850   1870   1890

Present era (PE)

1789
French Revolution

1769
James Watt patents
steam engine

1848
Revolutions in Europe

18ᵀᴴ CENTURY
Age of Enlightenment
(reason as principle of
philosophy and government)

1791
Death of Wolfgang
Amadeus Mozart

1870
Franco-Prussian
war

1776
USA independence

1815
Battle of Waterloo

1870
Paris Commune
(first assumption
of power by the
working class)

1804
First steam railway in
operation in Wales

1861
Unification of Italy
(first parliamentary
assembly)

1814–1815
Congress of Vienna and
Treaty of Paris (end of
Napoleonic Wars)

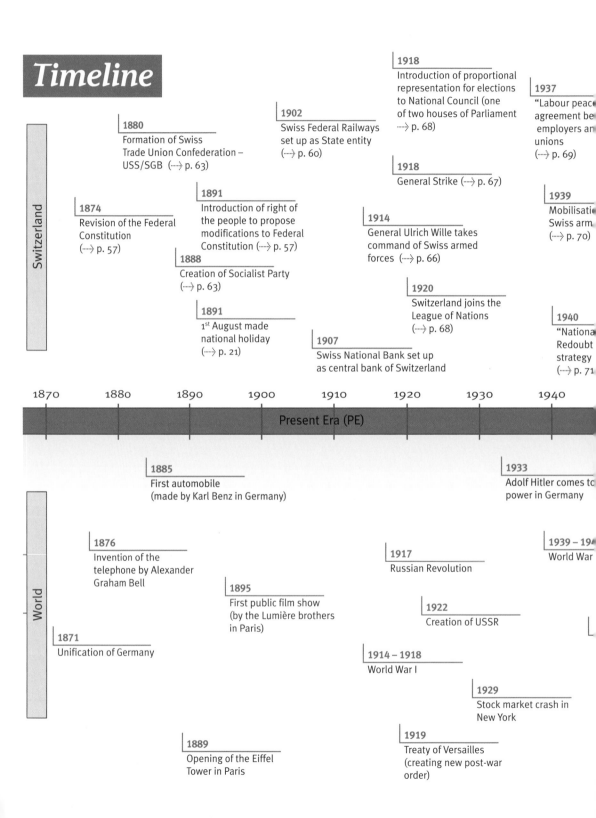

Timeline

Switzerland

1874
Revision of the Federal Constitution (----> p. 57)

1880
Formation of Swiss Trade Union Confederation – USS/SGB (----> p. 63)

1888
Creation of Socialist Party (----> p. 63)

1891
Introduction of right of the people to propose modifications to Federal Constitution (----> p. 57)

1891
1st August made national holiday (----> p. 21)

1902
Swiss Federal Railways set up as State entity (----> p. 60)

1907
Swiss National Bank set up as central bank of Switzerland

1914
General Ulrich Wille takes command of Swiss armed forces (----> p. 66)

1918
Introduction of proportional representation for elections to National Council (one of two houses of Parliament ----> p. 68)

1918
General Strike (----> p. 67)

1920
Switzerland joins the League of Nations (----> p. 68)

1937
"Labour peace agreement be employers an unions (----> p. 69)

1939
Mobilisatie Swiss arm (----> p. 70)

1940
"Nationa Redoubt strategy (----> p. 71)

1870   1880   1890   1900   1910   1920   1930   1940

Present Era (PE)

World

1871
Unification of Germany

1876
Invention of the telephone by Alexander Graham Bell

1885
First automobile (made by Karl Benz in Germany)

1889
Opening of the Eiffel Tower in Paris

1895
First public film show (by the Lumière brothers in Paris)

1914 – 1918
World War I

1917
Russian Revolution

1919
Treaty of Versailles (creating new post-war order)

1922
Creation of USSR

1929
Stock market crash in New York

1933
Adolf Hitler comes to power in Germany

1939 – 194
World War

1960
Introduction of compulsory
disability insurance (AI/IV)

1996
Bergier Committee set
up to re-examine
Switzerland's role in
World War II
(⤍ p. 74)

8
roduction of State
nsion system
S/AHV ⤍ see p. 67)

1978
Creation of the canton
of Jura (⤍ p. 79)

1959
"Magic formula" for
composition of Federal
Council (⤍ p. 78)

2002
Switzerland joins
the UN (⤍ p. 80)

1992
Swiss voters reject membership
in European Economic Area (⤍ p. 81)

1971
Women given right to
vote at Federal level (⤍ p. 78)

| 1960 | 1970 | 1980 | 1990 | 2000 |

Present Era (PE)

1957
First artificial satellite
("sputnik") launched

1999
War in Kosovo

1969
Establishment of
Arpanet, forerunner
of the Internet

1991
First Gulf War

2003
US intervention in Iraq

1957
Creation of the European
Economic Community
(future EU)

1989
Fall of Berlin Wall

5
mic bomb
pped on Hiroshima

1969
First man on the moon

1991
Abolition of apartheid
in South Africa

2001
9/11 attack on World
Trade Towers in New
York and Pentagon in
Washington, D.C.

1963
Assassination of
John F. Kennedy

1994
Rwanda genocide

1959–1975
Vietnam war

1995
Srebrenica massacre
in Bosnia

The 26 cantons

Switzerland comprises 20 cantons and 6 half-cantons (officially these are known as "cantons partagés").
N.B. Historically the half-cantons were frequently counted as one, hence references to the "Thirteen Cantons" and to Jura as the 23rd canton (⸱⸱⸱⸳ pp. 26 and 79 and maps 2 and 3 on pp. 38-39).

Aargau (AG)

Entered Confederation: 1803
Capital: Aarau
Population: 671,000
Surface area: 1404km²
Language: German

Appenzell Ausserrhoden (AR)*

Entered Confederation: 1513
Capital: Herisau
Population: 55,000
Surface area: 243km²
Language: German

Appenzell Innerrhoden (AI)*

Entered Confederation: 1513
Capital: Appenzell
Population: 16,000
Surface area: 173km²
Language: German

Basel-Country (BL)*

Entered Confederation: 1501
Capital: Liestal
Population: 287,000
Surface area: 517km²
Language: German

Basel-Town (BS)*

Entered Confederation: 1501
Capital: Basel
Population: 194,000
Surface area: 37km²
Language: German

Bern (BE)

Entered Confederation: 1353
Capital: Bern
Population: 1,031,000
Surface area: 5959km²
Language: German/French

Fribourg (FR)

Entered Confederation: 1481
Capital: Fribourg
Population: 315,000
Surface area: 1671km²
Language: French/German

Geneva (GE)

Entered Confederation: 1815
Capital: Geneva
Population: 495,000
Surface area: 282km²
Language: French

Glarus (GL)

Entered Confederation: 1352
Capital: Glarus
Population: 40,000
Surface area: 685km²
Language: German

Graubünden (GR)

Entered Confederation: 1803
Capital: Chur
Population: 198,000
Surface area: 7105km²
Language: German/Romansch/Italian

Jura (JU)

Entered Confederation: 1979
Capital: Delémont
Population: 73,000
Surface area: 839km²
Language: French

Lucerne (LU)

Entered Confederation: 1332
Capital: Lucerne
Population : 407,000
Surface area: 1493km²
Language: German

* Half-canton

Neuchâtel (NE)

Entered Confederation: 1815
Capital: Neuchâtel
Population : 178,000
Surface area: 803km^2
Language: French

Schwyz (SZ)

Entered Confederation: 1291
Capital: Schwyz
Population : 157,000
Surface area: 908km^2
Language: German

Valais (VS)

Entered Confederation: 1815
Capital: Sion
Population : 341,000
Surface area: 5225km^2
Language: French/German

Nidwalden (NW)*

Entered Confederation: 1291
Capital: Stans
Population : 43,000
Surface area: 276km^2
Language: German

Solothurn (SO)

Entered Confederation: 1481
Capital: Solothurn
Population : 270,000
Surface area: 791km^2
Language: German

Vaud (VD)

Entered Confederation: 1803
Capital: Lausanne
Population : 805,000
Surface area: 3212km^2
Language: French

Obwalden (OW)*

Entered Confederation: 1291
Capital: Sarnen
Population : 38,000
Surface area: 491km^2
Language: German

Thurgau (TG)

Entered Confederation: 1803
Capital: Frauenfeld
Population : 294,000
Surface area: 991km^2
Language: German

Zug (ZG)

Entered Confederation: 1352
Capital: Zug
Population : 125,000
Surface area: 239km^2
Language: German

St. Gallen (SG)

Entered Confederation: 1803
Capital: St. Gallen
Population : 505,000
Surface area: 2026km^2
Language: German

Ticino (TI)

Entered Confederation: 1803
Capital: Bellinzona
Population : 354,000
Surface area: 2812km^2
Language: Italian

Zurich (ZH)

Entered Confederation: 1351
Capital: Zurich
Population : 1,504,000
Surface area: 1729km^2
Language: German

Schaffhausen (SH)

Entered Confederation: 1501
Capital: Schaffhausen
Population : 81,000
Surface area: 299km^2
Language: German

Uri (UR)

Entered Confederation: 1291
Capital: Altdorf
Population : 36,000
Surface area: 1077km^2
Language: German

Switzerland (CH)

Federal City[1]: Bern
Population : 8,700,000
Surface area: 41,300km^2
Languages:
German/French/Italian/Romansch

Half-canton

[1] *The notion of capital city does not appear in official documents.*

Index